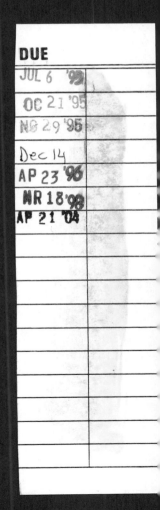

A Frozen Woman

A Frozen Woman

ANNIE ERNAUX

TRANSLATED BY
LINDA COVERDALE

FOUR WALLS EIGHT WINDOWS
NEW YORK / LONDON

A Four Walls Eight Windows First Edition

Copyright © Editions Gallimard, 1981
Translation Copyright © 1995 by Four Walls Eight Windows

Published by Four Walls Eight Windows
39 West 14th Street, #503
New York, N.Y. 10011

Library of Congress Cataloging-in-Publication Data
Ernaux, Annie, 1940-
[Femme gelée. English]
A frozen woman / by Annie Ernaux;
translated by Linda Coverdale.
p.   cm.
ISBN 1-56858-029-0
1. Ernaux, Annie, 1940-   —Biography.
2. Authors, French—20th century—Biography.
I. Coverdale, Linda II. Title.
PQ2665.R67F4713   1995
843' .914—dc20 94-45795
[B]   CIP

Printed in the U.S.A.

A Frozen Woman

$\mathcal{F}$ragile and vaporish women, spirits with gentle hands, good fairies of the home who silently create beauty and order, mute, submissive women—search as I may, I cannot find many of them in the landscape of my childhood. Not even in the next-best model, less elegant, more frumpy, the ones who work miracles with leftovers, scrub the sink until you can see your face in it, and take up their posts outside the school gates fifteen minutes before the last bell rings, all their housework done. Perfectly organized unto death. The women in my life all had loud voices, untidy bodies that were too fat or too flat, sandpapery fingers, faces without a trace of makeup or else slathered in it, with big blotches of color on the cheeks and lips. Their cooking skills did not go much beyond stewed rabbit and rice pudding, they had no idea dust was supposed to be removed on a daily basis, they worked or had worked on farms, in factories, in small businesses open all day long. There were the old ladies we visited on Sunday afternoons, with their boudoirs and the bottle of eau-de-vie to sweeten their coffee, wizened women all in black whose skirts smelled of butter going rancid in the pantry. No connection with those sugary grandmas in story books who wear their snow-white hair in a neat bun and coo over their grandchildren while they read them fairy tales. My old ladies, my granny and my great-aunts, they weren't nearly that chummy and didn't like it when you jumped all over them—they'd lost the habit. A peck on the cheek was all, at the beginning and end of the visit, so after the inevitable "You've gone and grown some more!" and "Still studying hard in school?" they really had nothing more to say to me, too busy talking with my parents in *patois* about the high cost of living, the rent, the lack of living space, the neighbors; they'd look over at me every once in a while, laughing. On Sundays in the summertime, we visited Aunt Caroline, biking along bumpy roads that turned into quagmires at the slightest shower, bound for the back of beyond—two or three farms and their pastures lying out on a plain. Caroline was never home, so after a perfunctory knock on the door, we'd check with the neighbors and eventually find her tying up bunches of onions or helping out with a calving. She'd come home, poke at the fire in her wood stove, break up some kindling, and fix us a light meal of soft-boiled eggs, bread and butter, and parsnip wine. A real wonder, that woman. "You're still bursting with health, Caroline! Aren't you bored, out here?" She thought that was funny. "What do you mean," she'd protest, "there's always things needing doing." Ever get scared, you know, all alone? That really surprised her, put a twinkle in her eye. "What could anyone get up to with me, at my age . . ." I didn't listen much, and slipping past the blind wall of the house, edged with nettles taller than I was, I'd go off to the pond to pick through the broken plates and tin cans my auntie dumped down there, all rusty and full of water teeming with bugs. Caroline would walk a little way along with us when we left, a good kilometer or so in nice weather. Then our bikes would leave her behind, a tiny dot in the fields of colza. I knew that this eighty-year-old woman, swathed in blouses and skirts even in the worst of the dog days, needed neither pity nor protection. No more than did Aunt Elise, swimming in her own lard but full of bounce, and a lousy housekeeper: when I crawled around under her bed my dress picked up dust pom-poms, and I'd inspect the dried crud on my spoon for a moment before daring to plunge it through the wrinkled skin of my poached pear. "What's the matter with you, you're not eating?" she'd ask, and her puzzlement would explode into a huge guffaw. "That itty-bitty pear isn't

going to plug up your fanny-hole!" Then there was my grandmother, who lived in a crummy prefab between the railway and
the lumber yard in the neighborhood called la Gaieté. Whenever
we arrived, she would be gathering greens for the rabbits or
doing some mending or washing, which irritated my mother.
"Why can't you take it easy, at your age?" Reproaches like that
exasperated my grandmother, who only a few years earlier had
been hauling herself up to the railroad tracks by gripping clumps
of grass, so that she could sell apples and cider to the American
soldiers after the Normandy invasion. She'd grumble a bit, then
bring in the pot of boiling hot coffee threaded with white foam
and pour a drop of eau-de-vie on the sugar stuck to the bottom
of the cups; everyone would swirl the brandy gently around.
They'd talk, nattering on about the neighbors, a landlord who
wouldn't make repairs, and I'd be a touch bored, as there was
nothing to explore in that little house without a proper yard, and
almost nothing to eat. My grandmother would slurp greedily at
the dregs in her cup. Her high cheekbones were as shiny as the
yellow boxwood egg she used to darn socks. Sometimes, when
she thought she was alone out in her scrap of a garden, she peed
standing up, spreading her legs beneath her long black skirt. And
yet, she had come in first in the *canton* on the exam for the primary school certificate, so she could have been a teacher, but my
great-grandmother had said not on your life, she's my eldest girl
and I need her at home to raise the other five. A story told a hun-

dred times, why her life hadn't come up roses. Once she'd been like me, running around, going to school, with no idea what was coming, and then disaster struck: with five youngsters to hold her back, she was finished. What I didn't understand was why she later had six of her own, without any dependents' allowances, either. You didn't need a map to figure out early on that kids—chicks, everyone I knew used to call them—put you truly in the hole, just buried you alive. And at the same time it seemed irresponsible, careless, the sort of thing you'd expect from poor people who had no common sense. Those large families I saw all around me meant swarms of runny-nosed brats, women pushing baby carriages and staggering along with bags of groceries, and constant griping at the end of every month. Granny had fallen into the trap but you couldn't blame her, back then it was normal to have six, ten children; we've come a long way since. My aunts and uncles were so fed up with big families that my cousins are all only children. I'm an only child, too, and an afterthought as well—that's what they call children born late in life, when a couple who hadn't wanted any (or any more) change their minds. I was their one and only, period. I was convinced I was really lucky.

The sole exception was Aunt Solange, poor Solange with that brood of hers, my mother always said. She lived in la Gaieté, too, and we often went there on Sundays. The neighborhood was like a vast playground where you could do anything you wanted. In

the summer, I'd join my seven cousins and their friends, shrieking on the seesaws we made from planks stacked next to the
lumber yard. In the winter we played tag in the one big bedroom
crammed with beds. I adored all this warmth and uproar, almost
enough to want to live there, but my Aunt Solange frightened
me. She was old before her time, always puttering in her
kitchen, her mouth twitching uncontrollably. Once she spent
months laid up in bed when her uterus decided to prolapse on
her. Then there were the times when she would get this vacant
look in her eyes; she'd open a window, close it, move the chairs
around, and bang, she'd start screaming that she was going to
take the children and leave, that she had always been unhappy,
while my uncle just sat calmly at the table, glass in hand, not saying a word or else sneering, "You wouldn't have any idea where
to go, you idiot." She'd rush weeping out into the courtyard,
threatening to throw herself into the cistern, but her children or
the neighbors would grab her first. As for us, we'd head tactful-
ly for the door as soon as the shouting started. Looking back, I
would see the youngest girl crying openmouthed, her teary face
pressed against the windowpane.

I don't know if my other aunts were happy, but they didn't
have that beaten-down air Solange had, and they didn't let anyone slap them around. With their red cheeks and lips, they were
always in a fever of activity, always in a hurry, with barely a
moment to stop on the sidewalk, clutching their grocery bags as

they leaned down to give me a little air kiss and rumble, "What have you been up to, my girl?" No fond displays of affection, either, none of those puckered-up mouths or cajoling looks people use to talk to children. These women were a bit stiff, abrupt, with tempers that exploded in swear words. At the end of family dinners, at First Communions, they would laugh until they cried, burying their faces in their napkins. My Aunt Madeleine would practically split her face in half, she'd laugh so hard. I don't remember ever seeing a single one of them knitting or patiently stirring a sauce; they'd serve cold cuts and other *charcuterie*, then produce from the pantry a pyramid of white paper stained with pastry cream. They couldn't have cared less about dusting and cleaning, although they made the ritual apologies, "Please, just pay no attention to the mess." Not domestic, these women, nothing but outdoor types, used to working like men ever since they were twelve years old, and not even somewhere clean, like a textile mill, but in a rope factory or cannery. I liked to listen to them, ask them questions about the whistle, the coveralls they had to wear, the forewoman, the times when they'd all be laughing together in the same room, and it seemed to me that they were going to school, too, only they didn't get homework or detention. At first, before I began to admire teachers, those awesome and superior beings, before I learned that watching jars fill up with pickles is not a great profession, I thought what my aunties did was a fine way to earn a living.

Towering over my grandmother and my aunts, those incidental figures, there is the woman all in white whose voice resounds within me, envelops me: my mother. Living with her, how can I not be convinced that womanhood is glorious and even be persuaded that women are better than men? She is strength and the tempest, but also beauty, and lively curiosity, a figurehead that opens the future for me, assuring me that one must never be afraid of anything or anyone. A woman who fights against one and all: the suppliers and delinquent payers in her business, the blocked storm drain in the street, the big shots always trying to keep us down. In her wake she carries along a soft-spoken, gentle man, a dreamer who mopes for days over the slightest annoyance but who knows heaps of silly stories, riddles ("Thirty-two white horses upon a red hill"), and songs he teaches me while he's gardening and I'm collecting worms to toss into the chicken yard: my father. I don't make any distinction between them in my mind, just that I'm her darling, his pet, their afterthought, and I must be like her because I'm a little girl, and I'll have breasts like hers, a permanent wave, and stockings.

In the morning, Papa-goes-to-work, Mama-stays-home, she-does-the-housework, she-prepares-a-tasty-meal, I drone along with the others, repeating everything without asking any questions. I'm not yet ashamed that my parents aren't normal.

My father doesn't leave in the morning, or in the afternoon, or ever. He stays home. He waits on customers in the café and the grocery store, he does the dishes, the cooking, the weeding. He and my mother live together in the same activity, with the men coming and going on one side, the women and children on the other, and all this makes up my world. They know the same things, they worry about the same things. He empties the cash register drawer every evening, she watches him count the take, and one or the other of them says, "Slim pickings," or sometimes, "A good haul." The next morning, one of them will deposit the money in their account. Not exactly the same work, true, there's always a code, but theirs owes nothing to tradition except the laundry and ironing for my mother, the gardening for my father. As for the rest, it seems to have evolved according to their personal preferences and abilities. My mother mostly looks after the grocery store while my father tends the café. On one side, the noontime rush, a tight schedule, customers who don't like to stand around waiting, women who want all sorts of things, a bottle of beer, a packet of Snowy pins, a wary crowd in constant need of reassurance—you'll see, this brand here is really much better. A performance, a line of patter. My mother emerges exhausted and beaming from her shop. On the other side, men spending hour after hour over a nice friendly glass, a quiet sit-down, no one watching the clock. No point in hurrying, no need to talk up the merchandise or even talk at all, since the customers hardly let you get a word in edgewise. Lucky for us, my mother says, who ought to know, because my father's a bit temperamental. Besides, tending the café still leaves him time for lots of other chores. When I finally wake up, to the music of pots and pans mixed in with songs and commercials on the radio, I go down to the kitchen to find him washing the dishes from the night before. He fixes my lunch. He'll be taking me to school. Cooking dinner. In the afternoon, he'll do some carpentry in the courtyard or slip out to the garden with his spade on his shoulder. It doesn't make any difference to me, he's always the same man, a bit off in the clouds, whether he's peeling pretty potato ribbons that curl between his fingers, grilling sausages that make our eyes sting with smoke, or teaching me how to whistle while planting leeks. A serene and reliable presence at all times. Compared to the working men in the neighborhood and the traveling salesmen who are gone all day, my father seems always to be on vacation, which suits me fine. On those Thursdays when my playmates insist that it's too cold for hopscotch in the courtyard, we play dominoes or a board game in the café. In the spring, I go with him to the garden, his pride and joy. He teaches me the funny names some vegetables have: Queen of Sheba onions, and a lettuce called Lazy Blondie. I help him stretch the string over the freshly turned earth. Together we put away a hearty lunch of cold meats and black radishes, turning over our plates to have a baked apple. On Saturdays I watch him kill the rabbit, then make it pee by pressing on its still soft belly. He peels off its skin with a sound like the tearing of old fabric. Papa-booboo who rushes in distress to inspect my bloody knee, goes to fetch the medicine and will sit for hours at my bedside when I have my chicken pox, measles, and whooping cough, reading *Little Women* to me or playing Hangman. Papa-chick, "You're sillier than she is," says my mother. Always ready to take me to the fair, to Fernandel movies, to make me a pair of stilts, to teach me some prewar slang, the cat's pajamas and other moldy oldies that tickle me no end. Indispensable Papa, taking me to school, waiting for me at lunchtime and in the afternoon, standing with his bike, a little apart from the throng of mothers, with bicycle clips on his pants legs. Upset if I don't appear right away. Later on, when I'll be old enough to come home by myself, he'll watch for my return. A father already getting on in years, amazed at having a daughter. In the unchanging golden light of memory, he crosses the courtyard, head bent because of the sun, a basket under his arm. I'm four years old; he teaches me how to hold the ends of my sleeves in my fists when I put on my coat so that my sweater doesn't bunch up around my armpits. Nothing but images of gentleness and solicitude. Householders whose word is law, loudmouthed domestic tyrants, heroes of the battlefield and workplace—I know nothing of you. I am my father's daughter.

Oedipus? I couldn't care less. And I adore *her*, too.

That deep, throaty voice: that's her. At parties, when it gets late, I fall asleep on her lap. Drafts, slammed doors—everything around her is always in motion, even exploding, like the ashtray that sails through the window one stupendous day to shatter on the sidewalk in front of the bewildered deliveryman who has made the mistake of forgetting some item or other. Just one of her fits of anger, the simple, reinvigorating kind: this business is for shit but for *shit*, she screams, and then peace, the jar of poppy-red candies that turn your tongue scarlet, the big box of assorted cookies the two of us plunder to console ourselves for her bad temper. I know, we know that she shouts for exercise, for fun, and that in reality she'll never get enough of being the boss. Even though it's only a small shop, she's still the boss. When she lets down her guard, she says she played her cards right after all. The store takes up about three-quarters of her time. She's the one who sees the salesmen, checks the invoices, figures out the taxes. Days of gloomy muttering when she sits at her paperwork, going over her additions in a low voice, licking her finger to thumb through the bills, and is absolutely not to be disturbed. An exception, this silence, because on other days she's surrounded by lively noise, the clanking of bottles, the clatter of the scales, stories of illness and death, when the only quiet moment is the little sum totted up on the Camembert wrapper or the kilo bag of sugar, then it's back to the latest news of who's dating, who's looking for work, who's going through the change of life. My first contact with the outside world is through my mother. My childhood features none of those homes where the only sounds are the faint tac-tac-tac of a sewing machine, the discreet noises of mothers who leave everything in apple-pie order as if by magic. Sometimes I go with other girls from my class to ring doorbells in the well-to-do part of town, along the rue de la République or avenue Clemenceau. Clutching our Tuberculosis Society stamps, we wait for a long time before the doors finally open only a crack, revealing timid women cowering in hallways filled with cooking smells, shadowy, depressing women who quickly shut us out again, displeased at having been bothered. As for my mother, she's the center of a vast network of women all telling her the stories of their lives (but only in the afternoon, when they do their shopping), of children who come in three times in one hour for two chocolate mice and one Malabar bubble gum, of old folks who are slow to pick up their change and the bags they've set down at their feet, steadying themselves with one hand on the counter. I never imagine she would do anything else.

"Mama is a *careful* housekeeper; she cleans house very *carefully*": double the *l* and add a *y*. What are they talking about? Housecleaning where I live is the Saturday tornado: the smell of Javel water, the café chairs upended on the tables, and my mother standing in a flood of water, her hair hanging down in her eyes, shouting at me not to walk on the wet floor. Around Easter time, it's the stale, chalky odor of roughly scrubbed walls, bedclothes piled in a corner, furniture pushed aside and stacked into shaky pyramids, and my mother on all fours scrubbing the parquet with steel wool. I can see her pink garters, and for days afterwards the chairs stick to our thighs. My father and I are intimidated by this tumult of water and polish, and all the commotion seems to exhaust my mother as much as it does us. Luckily I enjoy burrowing in the tunnel of rolled-up mattresses. And best of all, we go through this only once a year. The rest of the time, the cleaning is quite casual: a sheet to be ironed, the shop bell, a customer, and it's anybody's guess whether the sheet and the iron will still be cluttering up the kitchen table at the end of the day. At five in the afternoon she'll exclaim, "I've got a few minutes, I'll pull the spread up on my bed!" Her only obsession, as far as I know: the unmade bed. That and the obligatory laundry on Tuesday, when business is slow. A frightening ceremony that begins the day before with water lugged in from the outside pump so that the colored wash can soak in tubs all night. Then, disheveled and gummy with sweat, she toils as though possessed in the steam of the laundry room, and no one is allowed to go near her. She reappears around noon, wreathed in the sweetish smell of washing, mute, the personified hatred of I don't know what. But dust doesn't exist for her, or rather, it's something natural, not a problem. I feel the same way: it's just a dry veil powdering my cozy, a trail of lace when I take a book from the shelf, motes dancing in the sunbeams, something to be wiped off a vase or notebook with one's sleeve. Between twelve and fourteen years old, I will be amazed to discover that it's ugly and dirty, this dust I don't even notice. "Say, that hasn't been done in a long time!" remarks that snake Brigitte, pointing at a spot low on the wall. I look. "What hasn't?" My girlfriend shows me the thin top edge of the baseboard, all gray. She's right. You mean to tell me we're supposed to clean there, too? I'd always thought that was normal dirt, like fingerprints on doors and the yellow smudge over the stove. I'm vaguely humiliated by the realization that my mother is failing in one of her duties, since apparently this is one. Even later on, I'll be stunned to learn that we're also supposed to scrub the gas burner, the undersides of the sinks, the backs of the fridge and stove that no one ever sees—there's all sorts of stuff in women's magazines like *Femme pratique* and *Bonnes soirées* about how to make everything whiter and shinier, how to change your home into a bottomless pit of cleaning. And you're supposed to think it can be done quickly, in a twinkling. My mother's version of "quickly" is eating soup and then meat from the same dish to cut down on the washing-up, announcing brightly that this sweater doesn't look too dirty so why don't I wear it another day, letting everything get quietly dusty and worn.

She doesn't fool away time, as she puts it, on endless knitting. Occasionally, on a winter Sunday, as though seized with remorse, she tries to buckle down: the two of us laboriously count the moss stitches of a scarf that will never grow beyond twenty centimeters. The kitchen, that's *his* department, except for the inevitable pudding-from-a-package on Thursdays and the crêpes or fritters on holidays. The house smells festive from top to bottom, and the scent of spring is often in the air, too, since it's Shrove Tuesday or mid-Lent. The crêpes fly all afternoon as she offers them to the café regulars; my hands are glazed with sugar, my stomach is all upset, and we skip dinner that night. Or there's the cake mix for women in a hurry: "Clear your school-work off the table so it doesn't get filthy," and the mounds of powder collapse into the yellow sea of eggs. I am allowed to stick my finger into the batter for a taste. She lets me have half the raisins, and we both scrape the creamy bottom of the mixing bowl. During the next two weeks she won't crack a single egg. Cooking and cleaning are always the exception with her, depending on how she feels; you never know when she's going to do some polishing or wash down the walls, or maybe make a cake for a nice surprise.

And she still has the time, despite her bookkeeping and her customers and the shelves to be stocked, to get up at five when the mild weather begins so she can loosen the soil around the rosebushes and the sweet William, and she rubs my face with May dewdrops when I wake up. "It makes your cheeks bloom." Above all, any time, any place, buried in a book. That's where I find her superior to him, since he reads only the daily paper after dinner expressly to catch up on the local news. I envy her that strange, faraway look, withdrawn from me, from us, and the silence that envelops her, the absolute stillness that suddenly comes over her body. Afternoons, evenings, Sundays, she brings out a newspaper, a book from the public library, or sometimes even one bought in a bookstore. "I'm talking to you! How can you stand all those novels!" hollers my father. "Let me finish my story!" she answers back. I can't wait to learn how to read, so I can understand those long tales without any pictures she finds so enthralling. The day comes when the words in her books stop droning on and on and the miracle occurs: I'm not reading words anymore, I'm in America, I'm eighteen years old, I have black servants, my name is Scarlett, and the sentences are racing toward a last page that comes all too soon. *Gone with the Wind.* "How about that," she exclaims to her customers. "She's only nine and a half!" And to me she says, "It's good, isn't it?" I answer, "Yes." Nothing else. She is never able to explain much about what she feels or thinks, but we understand one another. From that moment on we share those imaginary lives my father ignores or despises, depending on his mood. "Wasting your time on lies, that's all it is." She informs him that he's jealous. I lend her my *Bibliothèque verte* series of classics, *Jane Eyre* and Alphonse Daudet's *Le Petit Chose*; she slips me *La Veillée des chaumières.* I sneak the ones she won't let me read from the cupboard: de

Maupassant's *Une vie* or Anatole France's *Les dieux ont soif*. Together we windowshop at the bookstore on the place des Belges; sometimes she asks, "Want me to buy you one?" It's like standing in front of the pâtisserie, gazing at the meringues and nougatines: the same longing, and the same impression of extravagance. "Tell me, would you like one?" The only difference from the pastries is that the bookstore owner does the picking and choosing, obviously, because outside of the popular romances of Delly and Daphne du Maurier, she's in unfamiliar territory. The store smells dry, a trifle dusty, pleasant. "Give it to my daughter," she says before paying. She promises that later on I can read a wonderful book, *The Grapes of Wrath*, and she either doesn't know how or doesn't want to tell me about the novel, leaving it for "when you're more grown-up." It's splendid to have a beautiful story waiting for when I'll be around fifteen, like my period, like love. One of the reasons I'm eager to grow up is the right to read any book I want. Neighborhood Bovarys, silly women lost in their idiotic daydreams, they're all hopelessly romantic, it's a fact——but why does it bother men so much, even my father, and later on, when my husband sees me sitting idle in the evening, he'll want to know what the hell I think I'm doing, dreaming my life away like that. Papers to correct, the kid to put to bed, barely five minutes left for reading before it's time to sleep. How can I keep on dreaming . . . It's true that I'll feel guilty, as though I were being lazy by not being "busy." No, my mother doesn't confuse her store with the coast of California, and the serial-story magazines she slips under the ironing when the shop bell rings never keep her from doing her bookkeeping. I know that soon I'll have to follow in the footsteps of those sweet, well-brought-up young ladies of *La Vie en fleurs*, and the *Brigitte* series in twenty volumes, *to be continued*, all those slaves or queens whose stories begin at eighteen and end with marriage at twenty, even my indefensible Scarlett with her scads of dresses and beaux. At the other end of the spectrum are those lurid, large-print, true-life confessions in magazines like *Confidences*: unhappily married women, seduced and abandoned girls, the massive chain of inevitable feminine tragedy that fascinates me terribly when I'm around ten years old. Women's reading: the bizarre idea that you have until you're twenty to succeed in life—perhaps that's why I'll prove so spineless on the terrace of the Café Montaigne and later on. No. I think the way people look at you is stronger than any old books, and I hate that insult men use: "You're letting yourself get carried away, you're just imagining things," poor girl—a good way to disguise all sorts of dirty tricks, to excuse missed rendezvous. "No, I'm serious, you've really got way too much imagination." Well, I could never wish for a mother whose face would not light up over books and magazines and newspapers, who wouldn't treat herself every week to a little vacation worlds away from the canned goods and the customers on credit, all that cold packaged grub, a mother who would think that reading was just plain rubbish. My mother tells me, eyes shining, "It's good to have an imagination." She prefers to see me reading, talking to myself in my games, writing stories in last year's school notebooks rather than cleaning up my room and endlessly embroidering a dish towel. And I remember her favorite reading as an opening on the world.

Too young to identify with eighteen-year-old heroines, I invent some family connection or acquaintance that allows me to traipse after them—off to those castles and exotic places and torrid tropical climes—as my very own self, with which I'm quite satisfied. Books: travel and foreplay. Delly's *Le Secret du Koo-Koo-Nor* turns my parents' bedroom into a Chinese boudoir, thanks to blankets and spreads draped over the chairs and window, while pillows piled on the linoleum become "voluptuous" cushions. My corvette is about to sink in a storm at sea, the chair balanced on the bed is tipping dangerously, and I'm Pedro, the little emigrant. My mother comes in, takes a look at the messy bed, at her Sunday dress dragging around my ankles, and says laughingly, "You're playing? That's good, have fun."

Reading, playing, dreaming, but every Sunday, and sometimes on Thursdays, also going off to explore the streets and sights around town. Not forgetting people, as though we don't see enough characters every day as it is. My mother feels the need for more, all sorts of pathetic wrecks, losers, old folks, invalids who will never get better, who got a foot caught in a

machine, who cracked up on a bike in a drunken stupor. My
mother has no idea that children should be protected, cocooned,
that their tender sensibilities should never be bruised, that cease-
less vigilance against marauding germs is required. She takes me
everywhere with her, to visit old Alice who has no sensation in
her legs all wrapped up in a blanket, and a faith healer may well
have told her she's on the mend, but I doubt she can even feel
herself pee. Old man Merle in his one room with grubby sheets
on the bed and cats clustered around a dish of scraps. The mothers of newborn children in the neighborhood, women secretly
ravaged in mysterious ways. It's nice to go into strange houses
where there are always funny things to look at, oval engravings
of Lourdes, odd-looking vignettes on painted wood, a cuckoo
clock, dolls won at the fair, collections of those little animals that
come free in a packet of coffee. Lots of smells, too. I've no need
to learn from a dictation exercise that "each house has its own
odor," which sends my classmates into a flutter: what, you're kidding, you mean it stinks? In my opinion, they don't know diddle.
Our visits last a long time, so I get restless, wondering why they
don't turn on the lights at nightfall, watching their faces gleam in
the shadows. Once outside, my mother grips my hand. You can't
see your own feet on those roads without any streetlights. "It's as
dark as a blackamoor's bum!" she says, and I laugh. The nursing
home is interesting, too, with the chapel and those big staircases
like the ones in castles. The best way to live would be off in a

trailer, all by itself on the outskirts of town, near a quiet bridge where nothing ever crossed, neither cars nor trains. An old woman holds my mother's hand for a long time; then they play cards. On the way back I find out she was having her fortune told, how marvelous.

He hardly ever comes with us, our stay-at-home, and when he does he drags his feet, without even glancing at anything around him because he hates taking a walk for no good reason. And it's often for no good reason, just to look, to get a breath of air, have a chat, talk off the top of my seven-year-old head that my mother and I set out "hooked up," arm in arm. Off to the woods, to see the daffodils. Along nameless streets, puzzling streets (there is no school on the rue de l'Ecole, and why name the rue de l'Enfer after Hell?), city streets full of children who stop playing to stare as we pass, streets with lovely houses haunted by invisible beings behind lace curtains. Keeping our eyes open for something new and different: half-demolished buildings with their rooms open to the sky, advertisements painted on walls, bull's-eye windows in rich people's houses. Streets downtown at Christmas time, where we gaze ravenously at the crèche scenes and fir trees, finally sinking our chattering teeth into the delicate shell and swirling frosting of a chocolate éclair. There are exceptional days of astounding discovery: the trip to Rouen. We spend the morning in perfumed palaces—those huge department stores, le Printemps and Monoprix—and the afternoon in churches that are green on the outside, black on the inside. Near the cathedral, we stop in front of a store selling books about the devil and Ouija boards. I walk along the slippery pavement and for the first time I have the feeling I'm not myself anymore. "Look up," she says: a gargoyle stretches out its neck. Here we are on the stairs in Joan of Arc's tower, or in the basement of the musée Beauvoisine, the only ones viewing the disappointing mummies, or down in crypts gaping respectfully (and trying very hard not to laugh) at row after row of tombs belonging to people we've never heard of. And now here we are ordering unfamiliar dishes in a restaurant, waiting anxiously for my first coquilles Saint Jacques, and what if I don't like it and can't clean my plate, then the trembling island of scallops to be explored with spoon and tongue, followed by the fear we won't be able to pay for all this, but she calmly gets out the money, don't worry we're rich today. My father nods without a word when I tell him of our exploits in the big city. What is it that drives her out and about, always going to exhibitions, prowling through the quaint parts of town? Why does she act like some well-meaning social worker dropping in on loonies, cripples, and derelicts? Shouldn't a woman stay demurely at home with her husband and children? As though I would ever ask myself such questions, when I am convinced she is perfect. She teaches me that the world is made to be pounced on and enjoyed, and that there is absolutely no reason at all to hold back.

*G*ranville Road, Kenver Avenue, I'm improving my English, not much, but I walk miles on the outskirts of London, Highgate, Golders Green, I sit alone in milk bars drinking Bovril, I'm twenty years old, dazzled by this change of scenery, and there's more, strolling on the via Tullio, in the gardens of the villa Borghese—and here they are already, those rude jerks, those dream-spoilers, getting in the way with their "Fräulein, hey Miss, oh mademoiselle, oo-la-la! French, francesa," but all paths are still wide open. Like the ones after my exams, faceless roads stretching into the distance, where I savor a delicious feeling of absurdity. And then there are those orderly gardens in the suburbs where I walk to try and shake off our first quarrel: I'm not setting out in search of adventure anymore, but running away. A laughable flight lasting a few hours, the pretense of a grand departure that will only lead me back to the stable. Later on I won't be able to go out anymore if I suddenly feel like enjoying some fresh air—I couldn't possibly just leave the baby in his crib, and still later on, there will be no point in even thinking about running away, because it wouldn't do any good, and I'm stuck in the kitchen, shedding hot tears over a hot stove. A well-broken little horsey.

No, my childhood was not one long idyll; I remember the slaps she gave me when I tore my dress, my lies, wishing she were dead, choking with rage, the boredom when imagination flagged, thinking if only I had a sister, the desolation in the air at the end of days when we hadn't had too many customers, those fickle, wily creatures you often have to keep your eye on. All my fears of dying. But when I look back from womanhood to girlhood, I know that I was spared at least one shadow over my youth, the idea that little girls are gentle and weak, inferior to boys, and that they have different roles to play. For a long time, the only world I know is the one where my father cooks and sings nursery rhymes to me, where my mother takes me out to a restaurant and keeps the family accounts. No question of masculinity or femininity, words I would learn later on—just the words, without really understanding what they mean, even if I have been persuaded that what you've got in your pants makes a big difference, what a laugh, but no, seriously, did I ever pay for it, raised in that outlandish fashion, without respect for conventional roles.

I admit, I'm rather pleased to be a girl. Because of my mother, of course. And then, I get a good look at what a man's world is like, in the café. Four-fifths of them drink too much, talk nonsense, and kill themselves working at tough, dirty jobs on construction sites. Shouting, gesticulating, ready to take on anything and anyone, tongue-tied until they've had a snootful but afraid of no boss on earth once they're in their cups, their conversation is just hot air. The bad ones beat up their wives, the good ones hand them their pay envelopes and in return get their Sundays off to go chase after their youth at the bistro or on the soccer field. What women do, I can see for myself in the store, is much more important: they shop for all the food, for sewing thread, for a pencil and double-sided ruler when it's back-to-school time, never any wild extravagances—a can of crabmeat demands some serious thought. And to top it off, gripes my mother, they're always comparing prices so they can pinch every penny, but easy does it, because they're the ones who hold the purse strings, and when they buy a big box of butter cookies, they want to get their money's worth. A sense of responsibility. At least in the ones who "keep a proper house." I must have heard it a hundred times, this phrase that means so many things: not throwing money out the window, scrubbing the children's faces before sending them to the store on an errand (at least on Sunday), but also keeping one's man on a tight rein, not letting him drink up his wages or change jobs at the drop of a hat. And I vaguely sense that almost all women's problems come from men. I don't brood over this, since my role model is my mother and she's nobody's fool.

*B*eing a little girl is first of all just being me—always so big for her age, her face is a mite pale, but luckily she's got solid meat on those bones, bit of a tummy on her, won't get her waist till she's twelve or so. Without suspenders or a tight belt, says the dressmaker, that skirt won't stay up. "Suspenders, I want her to be comfortable." All my clothes have to be comfortable, and made of sturdy stuff so they'll last a long time. I'm completely unschooled in wheedling, affectations, coy smiles, and tenderizing tears. My mother disapproves of "fusspots" and thinks crying is simply putting on an act. "Waterworks? Then you won't piss so much tonight."

A little girl hungry for as much pleasure and happiness as she can find, without a care for the effect on others. Staying in bed on Thursday and Sunday mornings until I feel faintly nauseated in my burrow of blankets, watching myself prance naked in front of the mirror, reading while I eat bread slices spread with hot apple butter at noon on school days without waiting for my lunch, endlessly riding my bike in the courtyard between the beds of asters and the empty crates. My bike, the marvelous dream machine. I feel airborne on the saddle, bumping gently between the shifting ground and motionless sky, reeling off my exotic stories to the rhythm of the whirling footpedals. Playing in the summer with my cousins or some neighborhood girls at those elaborate games that begin in a fever of excitement and joyous cries, pause while we eat our lunch sitting astride the cross-beam of the seesaw, and become bogged down in arguments, fights, or what are prudently described at confession as nasty conversations, in the hope that the voice behind the grating will not demand details. Pretend christenings and weddings where we use up all our energy getting ready to play, and why did we ever start this game, so we lose interest and then it's time to scamper out into the street in search of new adventures. The most thrilling ones are swiping peaches and pears, and running into some boys we can holler at from a ways off, happily calling them squinty-eyed blubbery nitwits, so that at the first signs of pursuit we can shriek, "Mama, they're bothering us!" "You started it," she replies. The ritual climb up the rope in the playground: the rope goes around the right leg, the left foot goes over the right, your whole dress creeps up, you strain to reach the ring at the top of the beam before tumbling back to the ground, the rope burning like fire from ankle to thigh. I spit in my hands and then up I go and down I come again. Never any calm, unhurried games. In company, I talk loud and fast to make up for the solitary murmuring of an only child. As for the natural reserve of little girls, their modest demeanor and supposed timidity, I don't see any of that in either me or my playmates. The dainty darlings who play dolly's tea party and pick pretty flowers? We call them fraidy-cats and stuck-up prissies. We enjoy our exuberance, which school, with its staid amusements, its get-in-line-and-keep-quiet, does little to dampen. Screaming, hiding where no one will ever find us, getting all messed up, daring—that's the big word: I dare you to . . . ring old lady Lefebvre's doorbell, say that out loud, show your whatever, sneak that peach. I'm unaware that in another language, our high spirits are called vulgarity, bad manners, that properly brought-up young ladies do not shriek like fishwives or hang out in the streets, and that they say fudge or shoot instead of you know what. The bistro's working-class clientele and the generations of peasant women that came before me are not really conducive to the creation of a Goody Two-Shoes.

It isn't always easy to do what is expected of me. My mother gives me lots of dolls, true, but I detect a note of pity in her manner, as though she were making a concession to my tender years. Still, she hands them over with a good grace, since I am the one asking for them. I'm not allowed, however, to go out in the street with those ridiculous items, a baby doll in a carriage. The word for dolls in our local dialect is *drouines*, and my *drouines* stay home. A vague memory of invariably curly hair, blankly staring eyes, and lips that are never parted wide enough for me to stick in a morsel of food. A parade of them, lost, broken, and obstinately replaced. For the pride I take in showing them to my playmates, with such a lovely dress, and the crocheted bootees, and she cries! When the admiration dies away, I put her back in her cradle and go off to jump rope. I keep thinking a miracle will occur, that I will love the next one, and knit clothes for her, and not leave her in the back courtyard. Joy at the new arrival, anxious selection of a first name, careful preparations for the baptism. After that, there isn't much I can do with her. How do you take care of a dolly? I'm not real handy at sewing dresses and bonnets, and whenever I ask my mother for help, she tells me to buzz off. That cold face carefully tucked into her baby buggy makes me sad. Lying there motionless, and me so lively, with a hint of spring in the mild air caressing my arms (bare for the first time since the end of winter), and the taste of mid-Lenten crêpes on my fingers. I look at her, and I can't think of a single thing to do with her. Lonely child with doll. My dream would be for her to love me back. Her body is hard, her Kiss-Me-Red smile is empty. The only way to put some life in her is to torment her, put her through some of those metamorphoses that can't help but lead to trouble. It always starts with the hair: braids, shampoo, curlers. Haircut. The fatal progression. Because of that devastated head—poor little baldy—I feel I can do anything, toss her up in the air so she'll land in silly positions, skirts up around her ears, or hold her hand and whirl her around at the shoulder on the rubber band that passes through her chest. One-armed in two seconds. Then I can commit the ultimate sacrilege, digging out of her belly the salt-shaker thing that still coos "Ma-ma" when

I turn it over. With the small naked dolls called bathers, it's different. They look too much like babies, so any tortures would be obviously criminal. But they can wind up in some unusual situations as well; if only I dared reveal the part played one summer afternoon by my diminutive companion, a baby doll named Michel . . .

I don't play favorites with games, I like them all: skip rope, hopscotch, handball. Pass-the-thimble, where you pass something small from hand to hand; such disappointment when I'm not chosen, such pleasure when I am, feeling the token slip between my palms like a secret proof of friendship. Bike riding with both feet on the handlebars. Steal-the-bacon. Building houses from dominoes. Climbing trees. Some Sundays, in la Gaieté, I go out in the street with my cousins and the neighborhood kids and to my surprise, the boys ignore us girls. They fight among themselves, rolling in the wood shavings around the lumber yard, leaving the girls to watch. So I attack them, tickling and biting, but I cannot make them really play with us. What is it I shout that day? Perhaps one of their own bad words I send back at them in provocation. As I remember the scene, two fourteen-year-olds, big kids, turn toward me. One of the boys shouts to the other, WHAT'S TO BECOME OF THAT ONE! Contemptuously. Threateningly. I have an idea of what he means, because I often listen in on what men talk about in the café, but I can't think of a thing to say, can't fathom the hitherto unsuspected connection between liking to fight and saying bad words, as they do, and becoming a slut. I can still see myself, hurt and offended, but worst of all, I don't understand, don't even have the heart to jump on him and start punching.

What will become of me? I will become someone. I must. My mother says so. And to start with, I need a good report card. Saturdays she tallies up my tens in dictation and arithmetic but doesn't scold me for the inevitable four in sewing and "fairly good" in conduct. She raises her eyebrows at the slightest dip in my grades and won't let my father make any excuses for his daughter: don't I have all the time I need to learn my multiplication tables and conjugate my verbs? They never disturb me when I'm doing my homework—or playing my games—to ask me to set the table or dry the dishes. "Don't you worry about anything but your own little self," they say. Oh, the greatness of this gift, the beauty of those sacrificed older sisters, the charm of the helpful little girls who bring in the cracker tray when aperitifs are served—that sort of thing doesn't happen in my house, it's even frowned on. And a child's delight at thinking herself useful, the idea that if you keep your room neat and clear the table "nicely" you will be loved . . . Not for me. Responsible only for myself and my future. That's vaguely terrifying, now and again; it would be so much easier to please people by peeling vegetables and being sweet to everyone than by constantly working hard and doing well in school. Now and again—but not often. The gray, overcast sky of September, men's voices making a loud hubbub in the café, the asters humming with bees: almost time to go back to school. The future. I'm between seven and ten years old; I know that I was put on this earth to do something. There's no brother whose prospects would take precedence over mine.

I now realize that my mother's attitude was also a calculated one. Just because she doesn't belong to the middle class doesn't mean that her girl shouldn't aim high; she wants a daughter who won't go toil in the factories as her mama did, who'll be able to say shit to anyone and live a free life, and to my mother, education is that shit and that freedom. So nothing is asked of me that might hamper my success, no little chores or housework that would tire me out. And it's important that this success not be denied me because I am a girl. For my parents, becoming someone has nothing to do with gender.

And it doesn't require wearing a bridal veil, either. Patiently, persistently, they persuade me—and from an early age—that marriage is only another adventure, like going to school and earning a living, just as it is for a boy. During our walks, my mother provides all sorts of examples for me not to follow: little What's-Her-Name who was such a nice girl and so smart but she failed her *baccalauréat* exams because she was engaged, and another girl who set her heart on making a good marriage—left in the lurch. According to my mother, the town is swarming with dumbbells who have made a mess of their lives, and I can see that I will have to watch my step. Especially since my neighborhood isn't oversupplied with good examples. There is Mlle Dubuc, bent double by the weight of her huge briefcase as she gets off the train from Rouen, where she's in medical school. Mlle Jay, who teaches English at the public school; she buys her milk and a few other items from our store every day. Not a vast throng, true, but they're "mademoiselles," not little What's-Her-Name or the Whosis girl. "You should be well prepared for life before anything else." So naïve, my mother: she thinks that education and a good job will protect me from everything, including the power of men.

$\mathcal{g}$ have to say that there's something missing from her directions for living. Little girl raised in a permissive atmosphere, provided with a glorious self-image . . . Well, not quite. I'm on my own when it comes to my thingy, more warm and alive than my legs or belly; she calls it my "nooky." In my head I write out nucky/mucky/yucky. Dirty, something to hide. "Will you stop parading around in your slip—go cover your bottom!" To be washed quickly, with a stern expression. Floundering alone in the dark with my fear, and later my shame and the need to go after what feels good. I want to know, learn, understand, and I keep my ears open for any peculiar expressions the grown-ups use. I still feel disgusted when I think of my body when I was a little girl, my dreams and conversations with other children. I have completely blocked out that period, ever since adolescence. At fifteen, set on the idea of offering a boy my complete innocence all tied up in a ribbon: heart, body, and soul, and he, like a god, will enter me as though he were entering an empty house. Determined to forget those fumblings and childish games and to believe that pleasure will begin with him. Actually, the first time is in a dream, before I'm five. The church they sometimes take me to when there are grand processions is vast, dark, and I am alone. I feel like peeing in a nice way, tingling and sweet. I crouch at the foot of the big gleaming pulpit, and I want to go so badly that it burns inside me, but it doesn't spurt out. Then I notice the priest staring at me, in his two gowns, the black one and the very short one of lace. My desire becomes excruciating. Night falls.

I want to sweep away all shame, speak triumphantly of my discoveries, admire how cunningly I deceived the adults around me, the stubborn way I resisted the ideal of the angelic little girl and the inquisitions of the priest (a different one, not the one in the pulpit) whose breath stank in his confessional-box. Because it isn't sad or bad to have hunted instinctively for the secret of that mysterious longing by exploring the little red house enclosed within two white shutters, so disturbingly smooth and fragile, as though it had been flayed. A hidden picture. My uneasiness years later in front of those triptychs in the Prado, with their half-open panels. Red, white. The queen pricked her finger and blood fell upon the snow. Open the shutters. Cautious examinations, sometimes involving tea parties with the dolls, and when I look at them on other days, they seem to remember. Amid the commotion of the classroom when our first-grade teacher isn't there, Chantal twirls in front of drooly old Geneviève, her "feely-finger" pressed to her temple; flipping up her skirt, she pulls aside the crotch of her panties and quickly spreads the wings of her secret place. Down flops the skirt. "Come on, Geneviève, do it!" Geneviève, who's not quite all there, shakes her head, won't play the game. "Mustn't, it'll bleed." She's close to the truth; I also think it's an open wound right in the middle of the body, but one that neither hurts nor bleeds. Until I'm about nine, this image has no depth to it in my imagination. "Mine," as my girl cousins and playmates and I call it, never looks exactly like "yours." Some girls show, and others look; some let themselves be touched, others do the touching. I'm not sure which group I should be in; the second, probably, because I'm often the youngest in these sessions and haven't any novelties to show off. Brigitte has a pointy chin and gives fascinating and meticulous lessons in anatomy, her eyes flashing from beneath her constantly tumbling ringlets; she loves that, showing and telling about the real red that will come, the black already starting to appear. We don't know many names and never suspect that there could even be serious words for these things in the dictionary. Everything is "it." Soon we would get "it," we'd be "well-developed," as the grown-ups say, and later we could "do it." How scared we are of being discovered by our parents in the middle of one of these instructive sessions. I bet they'd send us to reform school! And we laugh bravely. Impossible to resist this curiosity about our bodies. Where in all this is the "nothing" allocated to us, although I do not yet know this, by boys? Everything, on the contrary. The seat of a marvelous story that comes to me in small fragments not easily glued back together, but do I even really try, since I'm not bothered by weird or incredible things—after all, it couldn't be a simple matter or adults wouldn't be making such a fuss about it. I make progress, thanks to whispered nuggets of information, furtive games, and the inquisitive contemplation of couples locked in each other's arms in public parks. It's impossible to separate the awakening of my body from this disjointed body of knowledge. My charming, well-bred friends of later years will tell me how they were taught everything all in one go: the little flower, the seed, sitting on mama's lap, and she calmly draws a pretty picture, everything is harmonious, and geometrical, too, it all fits together, description of the parts and detailed explanation of the schedule of operations. I don't envy them. They didn't get the personal instruction sheet, either, the only one that counts. My earliest memory, when I am four: a neighbor boy my age is standing next to me, hosing the wall, and someone whisks me away from this vision. The revelation of a tormenting difference that would later delight me at the age of eight, when it can be benignly studied—from afar—on a statue, the famous satyr of la Gaieté, or closer up on the younger brothers of cheeky playmates: "Fwancis, show us your widdler." Don't have to ask twice, whenever you want, except the game gets tiresome after a while. But giggles, always, when looking at the boys' thingummies, whereas the sight of ours turns us more serious than catechism class. Just mentioning theirs was hilarious: willie weewee, piddling peter, "pid" for short. And it was funny to slip it into harmless songs, as a challenge. "I betcha I will!" "You won't!" "Just listen!" Singing on the swing: "If he had a dick he'd be a lot more slick, but there wasn't any more so I showed him the door!" A curiosity, a plaything, almost ridiculous. My mother calls it the same name as those scraggly plants that grow in windowboxes, "miseries." "Cover up your misery, Grampa Milon, there are children around." For a long time, it seemed to me a useless thing, pure difference. Because men make babies with their fingers. The first version of the story to be acted out. The problem is, how long does it take, a minute or an hour? Never determined, not even when I reach the next version and learn what the misery is for. And all those marvelous doubts . . . A huge poster on the way to school intrigues me: a woman, lying down, with a man's head buried in her lap: "*Confidences*, the

weekly family magazine." My mother announces in the store
that ads like that are a disgrace. Can a man do it with his head,
too? And this knee grown-ups joke about, playing kneesies
under the table; that smooth surface says absolutely nothing to
me, but still, you never know. For a long time, everything takes
place on the surface, as far as I'm concerned, and I never suspect
any penetration can go farther than that tiny groove behind the
closed shutters. Even my "period" I imagine to be a series of
minute red polka dots that will one day spot my skin. Brigitte's
lessons must not have been too clear. The next version of the
story is quite startling. Do I guess or does someone whisper in
my ear? The memory is muddled now. It's the moist peepee-
hole, the one babies come from, that is used, not the little red
house. No more play-acting: the experience would be useless
and painful. For a while, I am perturbed by this discovery that
the important part of my "mine" is a hidden tunnel where I've
never felt anything, a silent and invisible hollow. The difference
now becomes clear, logical, and disconcerting. I curb my astonishment, as usual. During my childhood, for as far back as I can
remember, nothing ever shocks or worries or disgusts me. I
must have accepted the new arrangement and ignored any
uneasiness I felt over this unknowable part of me inside my body
so that I might think only of the promise of pleasure. "Doing it"
can't be anything else, the most important thing in the world,
an act that I unconsciously disassociate, naturally, from the ter-

rible consequences that are inevitably involved: having a baby. A skip-rope rhyme popular in the fourth and fifth grades, the year of our solemn communion: "First comes love / Then comes marriage / Then comes me / With a baby carriage." Never mind, first the pleasure—I always erase the rest of it in my fantasies. Childbirth, the only thing that fascinates me with horror because I learned about it in *Gone with the Wind*: the ropes, the hot water, and screaming your head off while you clutch the bars of the bed. Torture and terror. Dire rumors of difficult births requiring forceps, probably something like the pliers my father uses to get the tube off the wheel rim when he has to fix a flat on my bike. I always thrust aside that episode of my story, preferring to concentrate on more cheerful developments, the appearance of breasts, hair, and blood, marvels I watched for with keen curiosity. And it takes so long, especially for the last metamorphosis, this miracle that arrives without warning. For you know neither the day nor the hour, it just happens, and like all the things that are supposed to happen in my body, I never imagine any afterward. One day I'll be a girl with my period, I'll strut about in a halo of red glory, I'll go to sleep with my new self, and life will be close to reaching perfection. Except for childbirth, which resembles a punishment, I think of all my transformations as celebrations. I don't believe in the pain that makes some girls wince every month; my mother never complains, and I cannot associate the happiness of finally having "it" with stomach cramps. I am sure I will not suffer. And also that I will like to "do it." It isn't simple, the business that lies ahead, and I don't know much about boys, but I'm sure it will be fun. The bicycle bumps along over the dark ground in the courtyard where no grass grows, as I wind my way around the crates, drawing ever closer to my imaginary India and Argentina with every turn of the pedals, but closer as well to that glorious body of tomorrow for which everything will be possible. To travel and make love—I don't think anything seems more wonderful to me when I am ten.

The lines of the body and the heart should not be confused; the latter line tends to be somewhat dotted. Was I really a little girl in love? Do the boys—those objects of curiosity and obligatory partners of my reveries—have names and faces? I invent many of them from my reading. Charles, rejected by Scarlett, becomes my fiancé during the period of the sufficient and indispensable finger. In *La Semaine de Suzette*, a girls' magazine, I find fourteen-year-old heroes, just the right age, whom I accompany in search of treasure hidden in country houses off in Brittany. There are some real-life "sweethearts." My girlfriends pick out lots of them for me: you've got this one, and that Fouchet boy—I'm so proud, I sort through them and say which ones I like the best, swearing cross my heart that if I ever get the chance, I'll go all the way with that one. What chance. We say "Hi," that's it. Don't even dare use first names, that would be a sure giveaway. Can't remember the names, now. Most important are the ones I don't brag about. There's that sweet altar boy with the pasty complexion who accompanies the old lady, the pew attendant on the right side of the church. He appears, with downcast eyes, between the reading of the gospel for the day and the elevation of the Host; he wears a pretty surplice of lace over his red gown, which is a bit short, so I can see his shoes. He holds out his slender, damp little hand, into which I place my twenty-franc piece. I hold out my hand for my ten francs of change. Every Sunday I wait for a look, something, but my conquest is always a flop, and God and the Virgin aren't helping. I don't yet understand that simply being there is not enough to attract attention, you have to turn on some charm, be a bit flirty—and how dumb can you get, throwing yourself at the boys like that, they want to be the ones making the moves, etc. All the tactics I'll learn about later on. Now for the guys I boast about. A tall boy who has just gotten his primary school certificate is over at my house, when suddenly he grabs me violently from behind with one arm, plants his lips on my neck, and dashes off. This confuses me. I have not felt faint at the touch of "his burning kiss," delivered while I was watching our bunnies nibble the crackers I had brought them. Perhaps I was not prepared for this event. But anyway, that's it, I can tell everyone I've been kissed. Then there's the one whose name is sheer magic for years. Simon. Black eyes, white teeth, sparkling smile, it sounds like a soppy love song but that's him, plus his white shorts set off his nice brown thighs. We roller-skate together one whole afternoon and he never falls once. Summertime. We say good-bye on the road into town. I wait for the bus with my father. I can see the beginning of the street where Simon lives from the bus stop. We wait a long time. I look at the asphalt on the road, the empty lots sporting rusty pieces of junk, and the factories in the distance, making a sound like the roar of the sea. I'm unaware that this is my first scene of parting. I think I'll be coming back the following year. "Simon says raise your arm; Simon says take a step." He's the one speaking to me through that girl on the playground. I write his initials everywhere. And still the same thing, even further back. They've taken me to hear a military band on the place des Belges: cloudy sky the color of smoke; a sea of backs huddled in rough woolen coats. Among all the heads I notice the nape of a soldier's neck. He's blowing away on a bugle, I think. Sometimes I see the hint of a profile, or he puts an arm down. I keep coming back to that skin between the razor-straight line of his hair and the khaki collar. I do not stand there endlessly scraping the toe of my shoe along the ground, or trying to see patterns in the gravel, or imagining a tiny house between people's feet—all the things you do when you're stuck in one place. That day, gazing at that neck, I understand what happens between a man and a woman, what all Brigitte's descriptions never make me feel. Something luminous. Nothing to do with toilet talk. The first real presence of a man.

On vacation, out in the courtyard under fluffy white clouds, I'm swinging, talking to myself. The cases of empty wine bottles give off a musty smell. A customer drops by the café; in her white smock, my mother busies herself over by the shelves. I hear a steady metallic pounding from a workshop, the piercing whine of a power saw, the rumble of trains on the tracks nearby. Men are the movers and shakers of the world around me: they build roads and repair motors, while women make only discreet noises inside houses—the knock of a broom against a baseboard or the murmur of a sewing machine. I am ten years old, and like all little girls, I have no idea of this. The surrounding hum of the city means nothing to me. Nestling inside it is my existence, precious to me and my parents. The world of boys doesn't threaten me. Nothing but an intermittent dream, a promise of happiness. Neither bright light nor shadow, not yet.

*Y*ears that I thought were full ones. Illusion. Undermined, no doubt, by second thoughts, the sly smiles of prudes, religion, the discovery of other role models. My spinster schoolteachers never make as deep an impression as my mother does, but they, too, are strong, active women, all-powerful, with hands that write difficult things on the blackboard, and a way of waiting with that set look on their faces, arms crossed: "Be seated and be quiet." They know everything, and even though I don't love them because they seem so strange to me, with their words and their refined manners, I admire them. It doesn't bother me at all that women are more knowledgeable than men. The men I see at school wear long black dresses like my grandmother: the chaplain and the priest. The headmistress drags this last through the classrooms each trimester to hand out grades. He beams moistly at us, just a touch gaga, in contrast to the flushed and furious principal who is always ready to explode at our laziness and stupidity. Of course she's the one who counts. I've no reason to fear her as far as grades go. A good reputation, the truly narcissistic high opinion of oneself that this provides, scholastic success. Freedom, self-confidence. A taste of power, obviously. The teachers overlook my rambunctiousness, which stays with me for a long time—an only child so thrilled to find twenty playmates to chatter with, even if half of them are show-offs and crybabies who wail at the slightest bump. The other half, neither as well dressed nor as well mannered—they're enough to make me happy. Our dear ladies couldn't make ends meet with just the uppercrusters, so they have to take on the daughters of farmers because it pays good money, and then they round out the list with girls from working-class families with big ideas. Elisabeth, who comes to class in winter with her mother's stockings sewn to her panties, and Chantal, who is such good company downtown after school. Together we buy Raymond Radiguet's *The Devil in the Flesh* because of the cover. Bernadette, a champion at giving the teacher impudent looks from under her bangs—don't you be rude young lady! Unfazed. My pals. They don't often win the cross, the handsome copper medal awarded on Saturdays to the most deserving, the diligent, the obedient, the fakers who can smell the teacher coming a hundred meters away and snap into angelic poses. The headmistress awards the medal in person, with a kiss. You should see them glow, the winners. On Monday they wear it to school pinned to their blouses with a superb bow with two, even four fat loops of ribbon, a real flower. Some of them must polish the thing with Twinkle. I have a terrible knack for it. They keep on giving it to me, "although you certainly don't deserve it, my dear, for your behavior. Or for neatness. Remember," says the head, fixing me with a stern eye, "one may receive tens in everything and yet not please the Good Lord. Once there was an extremely gifted little girl—not one of you could have held a candle to her—who passed all her exams brilliantly, every one of them. Do you know what she is now?" Deep silence. I'm still standing there waiting to get the cross. "They push her around in a wheelchair. She has the mind of a two-year-old. Because of a disease sent to her by God." For one moment—no more—I wish I were at the very bottom of the class. Even if God obviously doesn't care about grammar or arithmetic, my mother does, while marks for good conduct and pretty drawings in our notebooks, in her opinion, are cat piss. The cross? Stuff and nonsense. Besides, I keep losing it, and my mother hates having to hunt through the cupboard drawers and find it wedged between some cookie boxes. No pretty ribbon bow. "I haven't time for that! Study hard, that's the main thing." Under these conditions, it's difficult to believe everything the headmistress says.

The pleasure of being thoroughly myself when I recite a poem, conjugate a verb, or solve a math problem without a single mistake. Strength. Support and comfort in the face of the fact that the teachers clearly prefer certain students, the ones I call show-offs, daintily dressed, with curls, a little barrette here, a white collar there, mother's little darlings. My braids are pinned on top of my head, no hair in my eyes, it gets in the way—one of *my* mother's unshakable principles. The sweetie pies, the cute pixies, they're just naturally charming, that's what I figure. The ones the teacher in charge of school plays, pageants, and all the other festive hopping-around put on to entertain the families inevitably picks when she shows up in the classroom to muster her troops. "I need six daisies for 'The Waltz of the Flowers,' stand up, girls, let's see—you there, you'll do nicely." Usually it's the same ones. I have hopes, at first. Too bad, maybe next year. Once I was picked and sent back two minutes later. I'm always too big, no matter what class I'm in, too clumsy, paralyzed at the idea of moving my arms and legs around while people are watching. Rejected. The chosen ones enjoy their special status for weeks; they are fetched for rehearsals right in the middle of class and receive mysterious messages: "At one o'clock in the assembly hall." Finally, they appear one evening under the lights, in spotless tutus, revealing their secret identities as living dolls. If I'm not a doll, then what am I?

Quick, come to me, my make-believe appearance, the one I invent for myself when I'm bored in school, taking Roseline's long blond hair ("It would be a crime to cut it," the teacher says), Françoise's round, rosy cheeks, the slim figure of Jeanne, a young Greek goddess (I'd read that somewhere). The only thing of mine I keep is my eyes: they're nothing special, but I'm attached to them. Secretly I'm already busy with the next installment of the outlandish story I tell myself to replace the real girl with a paragon of grace and delicate beauty. Before the bell at half past one, the big girls of twelve and older are talking, laughing; one of them wears red ankle-boots and a blue blouse. I adore her because I'm going to be like her, and I'll press the back of my hand to my forehead the way she does and exclaim, "Algebra, what a drag!" I possess nothing like her round face and slender limbs, but I'll get there, at the same time as I get to the algebra.

I love looking at her, which isn't easy; the others flock around her, hiding her from view, but she reappears, unaware of my existence, because big kids don't give a damn about little ones. I never identify with tall, sturdy girls or ones who have boyish features, who don't conform to the standard image of the pretty little girl. Rolande, my deskmate for one whole year, resembles a shepherd out of a book of Bible history. Her pale mouth whispering next to my ear repulses me. Vague and awful suspicion: sometimes there's not a great deal of difference between boys and girls, physically. Yet many of my classmates fall into this blurred category—why does it upset me? I must already have it firmly in my head that girls are supposed to be all gentleness and soft curves. All these faces among which I seek my own . . . No, at ten years old, I am not yet as complete a person as I would have liked to be.

Although they aren't brutal about it, our teachers do their bit—under a sugarcoating of religion—to erode our will and self-confidence, as though they were denying us the same favor they had themselves been granted, to teach and make their own ways in life. I remember everything: my astonishment and disbelief, and the teacher—Sylvestre is her name, she can't stand me, always reprimanding and making fun of me. She looks like Saint Thérèse of Lisieux, with her hair caught up in a barrette and hanging down her back. All bubbly, that day: "Tell me, girls, what would you like to be when you grow up? A farmer, yes; a secretary, that's very good." And she asks us why, helping us with our answers. She cuts me off short: "You'll run a grocery store like your mother, surely!" I can't get over it; I'd been going to say, "Teacher." Well, she must know better. Too bad. Now it's Marie-Paule's turn: she's calmly grinning from ear to ear. "And you?" "Me, I'm going to be a mama." Howls of laughter from everyone, even the little prigs; we are all collapsing on our desks, looking around at one another, because that makes it twice as much fun when you laugh. A furious Mlle Sylvestre barks at us, "Be quiet, you little imbeciles!" She begins to speak softly, slowly sweeping her stern gaze across our upturned faces. "Being a mama, for your information, is the most wonderful job in the world!" No one bats an eye. Farmer, doctor, we've even had a nun, grocer— all that goes out the window. I still remember my total incomprehension. Perhaps because this is the first time anyone has ever thrown all my convictions into confusion. She has a real gift, Saint Sylvestre de Lisieux—two truths for the price of one: a grocer's daughter I am, so a grocer's daughter I will always be, besides which, there is no destiny more glorious than pushing brats around in a baby carriage.

"Don't bother your head with that, just study." My mother sets me straight again. Coercive, but reassuring. Yet they must have had some effect on me, those twelve years of listening to my teachers harp on and on in praise of sacrifice and selflessness. The body is a cesspool, intelligence a sin. The prayers aren't the worst of it, but oh, the lives of the saints: Agnes, that white lamb, whipped, tortured, fed to the lions; Blandine, the same scenario; Maria Goretti, a knife plunged right in the heart, and I weep in class over Joan of Arc. Bernadette was almost illiterate, girls, but do you know, that poor, modest shepherdess was chosen by the Good Lord, even though He could certainly have picked someone much more educated, and the three children of Fatima, and the two humble shepherds who saw the Virgin at La Salette, blah blah. Fascinating. Simplicity, innocence, the mortification of the body, and even the *ne plus ultra*, martyrdom, like the scrofula afflicting Saint Germaine. These women sacrificed their lives, and nothing, girls, could ever be more pleasing to God than that. Sucking blissfully on caramel lollipops, tackling the climbing rope, whispering in line—all that is vaguely sinful. The leitmotif is making sacrifices: for example, not talking even though you'd like to; going without dessert; doing the dishes for your mama. Whenever you don't want to do something, do it. Keep a notebook and write your sacrifices down. Some girls fill their notebooks with numbered lists. Emulation in renunciation. Maybe it's the same song and dance in the religious dumps for boys, the same régime of purity and fear, but they can't be kept down as much as we are—they're allowed to fight, encouraged to become leaders, and the good fathers don't despise balls, *duas habet*. I become convinced early on that women are more pious than men: they pack the church on Sundays, while my father waits for Low Sunday to go to confession and take the sacrament at Easter time. He hates the whole business and only goes at all to avoid a huge scene at home. Women *have* to be more pious. If a man isn't religious, it doesn't matter, because we girls are here to save the world through our prayers and exemplary behavior. Luckily I feel overwhelmed, utterly unworthy despite all my efforts, and my sacrifices do not fill me with the anticipated happiness. I'm careful to hide my infamy: the joy I feel at racking up those good grades, seeing things I'm not supposed to, pinching candies from my mother. My natural naughtiness. My sloppiness, simply impossible to hide: smudges on my notebooks (how can I explain that I do my homework on the kitchen table?), fingerprints on my sewing squares. "Cleanliness is next to godliness, mademoiselle!" I am exposed. Stain—that troubling word. The stainless virtue of Mary. How can I ever conceal all the violence and longing I trundle about inside myself? It's so hard, with a guardian angel at one's back and God everywhere, and one's conscience, that big staring eye floating up in a corner of the ceiling, the first lesson in the ethics book. During our catechism sessions in the freezing chapel, I try vainly to hide in the back rows with all the gigglers, but the headmistress makes sure I do not escape the attention of the bespectacled chaplain. And the Friday confession slips, an awful custom. We write our names on pieces of paper that the teacher collects and sends to the priest. Later, when we are plumb in the middle of a geometry problem, a student will enter and hand a slip to the teacher, who stops the class to read the name out loud. So that we all know who is scrupulous enough to wish to be pure and spotless in the eyes of God. How proud they are, getting up to leave the class-room, returning twenty minutes later with another piece of paper and another name. The daisy chain of good little girls. The secret shame of staying seated, noticed immediately by one's teacher and classmates. Once a month, crawling with revulsion, I join the chain. But resistance is best, and silence. All in all, I prefer the guilt of hidden transgressions to that atrocious, flac-cid moment after confession. Kneeling between the statues of Saint Cecilia and Saint Lawrence, I hate having admitted to the priest that I have committed the sin of pride, that I have stolen plums and sung dirty songs. That nervous tongue wetting thick lips, that fetid curiosity—I just hate myself. Little girls must be transparent to be happy. That's too bad. Me, I feel I'm better off in hiding. Convinced that this attitude will carry me through, I protect myself from within, with a solid dark core of wicked-ness and desires. This same defense mechanism also means that I am scared witless that the Virgin will appear to me, and then I'll have to become a saint, which doesn't appeal to me one bit. I want to travel, to eat papayas and rice with chopsticks, and use what gifts I have to become a doctor or a teacher. So whenever they lecture us, I use some and leave the rest behind.

One always leaves less of it, however, than one thinks. Especially since it's difficult, even impossible, to figure out all the connections involved, like the one between that admiration they instill in us for the Virgin, the mother of us all (and the Church is our mother as well), and the respect we owe to "your dear mama." I hope that you help out at home, girls, because you could never show her enough gratitude! Who does the cleaning? She does. Who irons your dress? She does. And the meals, and so on. And on. It's a heavy burden, the maternal iconography dispensed by the good sisters. "When you distress your mama, she goes off all alone and cries." The two streams of tears running down the Virgin's cheeks. "Whatever would become of you without your mama?" The teacher's tone grows threatening. I imagine the earth as a wasteland where I wander blindly, alone in the world. I still feel a cloying anguish when I recall the singsong of those voices, so horribly sugary and tragic. Do your very best to show your gratitude. Embroidered doilies, raffia baskets, sashes of corded cotton—we start getting ready right after Easter, spending the end of every afternoon busily working on our Mother's Day presents. The whole thing is a joke to me, a kind of school holiday; needle in hand, I have a wonderful time listening to stories and telling some myself, taking a stitch about once a minute. Suddenly, the icy reprimand: "Mademoiselle, I have my eye on you. You aren't doing a thing and you will never finish your doily in time!" I feel like blurting out the truth, of which I am quite certain by the age of eleven: my mother doesn't care a hoot for her present, she will spend the entire morning of the Sunday in question running from one end of the shop to the other, and the small package placed between her napkin and the plate of canned sardines will embarrass her no end. "Oh, how sweet of you. Let me give you a little kiss!" And then, "Let's put it away so it doesn't get dirty." That's the end of that. No question of me reciting the short poem we've all been taught—the two of us would feel absolutely ridiculous. I'd never dare admit such things, especially when the teacher announces in front of the whole class, "If you don't finish your doily, it means you do not love your mama!" I beaver away at my embroidery, convinced that I'm a monster, even if Mother's Day in my house is a load of poppycock.

On such occasions, I have the disquieting feeling that my mother isn't a real mother, one like all the others. Neither weepy nor coddling, still less house-proud, she is someone I do not often recognize in the composite picture provided by the teacher. That spirit of self-sacrifice, the perpetual smile, and that deference toward the man of the house—imagine my surprise and skepticism (but not too much embarrassment yet) when I don't see any of these traits in my mother. And if the teacher only knew that she uses bad language, and sometimes leaves the beds unmade all day long, and tosses customers out of the café when they've tied one on too tightly! And it's so irritating, the way the teacher whispers "your ma-*mah*"; at home and all around my neighborhood, we say "*ma*-ma." Big difference. That ma-mah stuff is for other mothers than mine. Not the ones I know well in my family or among our neighbors: always in a complete snit, griping about how children don't come cheap, walloping kids right and left to keep them in line—it's just unbelievable how much they lack that "inner glow" so characteristic of the ma-mahs our teacher describes. I see *them* after school, when I go to meet my father, who waits for me with his bike. Elegantly dressed, refined ladies. The kind referred to in fashion magazines as "the mistress of the house," who simmer delicious dishes in their cunningly decorated homes while their husbands are busy at the office. I see the ideal mother as part of a way of life that has precious little to do with ours.

Marie-Jeanne isn't a very good friend of mine, but one day in June she invites me to her nice house, with its small garden, to have a glass of lemonade. We are going to sell raffle tickets together on her street. The dark hall, hung with paintings, opens onto a gleaming white kitchen like the ones in catalogues. A slender woman in a pink blouse moves quietly between the sink and the table. A pie, perhaps. Through the open window, I catch a glimpse of flowers. The only noise: tap water running gently over strawberries in a sieve. Everything is clean. Bright. Neat. A woman light-years from my mother, the kind of woman to whom a child could recite a Mother's Day poem without feeling silly. A sleek woman, and happy, I think, because everything around her seems lovely to me. In the evening, Marie-Jeanne and her brothers will calmly eat the meal prepared for them, like a scene of domestic harmony from the moralizing poetry of Sully Prudhomme, without any shouting or the anxious counting of money on a corner of the table. Peace and quiet. Paradise. Ten years later, I will be the one in a silent, sparkling kitchen, with flour and strawberries: I have stepped into the picture, and it's killing me.

Anyway, until my adolescence, it doesn't strike me as strange that my father washes the dishes and my mother lugs around bottle-racks. Cooking, sewing, and ironing are not high on my list of values, or anybody's, for that matter, since at school they send the hopeless dummies dozing in the back of the class off to "home economics," in a classroom up under the eaves. The ten-year-old ballerinas in their tutus give me a brief pang, but out in the courtyard I fly high on my swing and ride my bike while I dream my dreams. I have energy to burn, my mother says. Doesn't matter if I'm pretty or ugly, graceful or not: I love to watch myself in the mirror in my Rosebud panties and slip, capering around to music only I can hear. Soon I will be twelve years old. One summer night, unable to sleep, my face pressed to the window, I see the sun rise for the first time. When the darkness has paled to the light of day, I fall asleep in the astonishment of a strange and precious discovery, as though I have done something forbidden. Still happy and free, that year.

*I*n a few years I will become a girl emptied of herself, swollen with romantic ideas in a world reduced to other people's expectations. My defenses crumble. I remember the summer when I was twelve, and I can already see the first signs of this collapse: my growing interest in the love stories my mother reads and the most sentimental songs on the radio, the melting "*Etoile des neiges*," and "*Boléro*," with guitars singing beneath a red and black sky. Then there is my discovery that men are interested in girls who are "curvaceous," and especially interested in their thighs when they're wearing shorts. When Claudine goes down the street, the workers on scaffolds whistle, and she's only two years older than I am. I worry. Will I be considered curvaceous? I'm putting off reliving my adolescence. I can already tell that I'll be cheating, praising everything that seemed so unspeakable and lousy at the time (my real body, pleasure, my fleeting realization that I am not a truly feminine girl) and ridiculing all that I found so wonderful, like being noticed by boys, having a certain look or style. I'm going to say that the romantic daydreams that filled my thoughts during math class are so much twaddle. I'm writing myself and can do as I please: I can turn myself in any direction I like and easily put new words in my mouth. But if I'm trying to show clearly the path I took to become a woman, then I shouldn't spit on the great lump of a girl weeping with rage because her mother won't let her wear stockings and a revealingly tight skirt. I should explain. Without calling myself a fool. Are those years even over? It probably goes back to when I was fifteen, that fear I have of seeing myself in a mirror before I've had time to adjust the eyes and smile, putting on my best face. I'm still looking for the reflection of an imaginary body, the one that began to dance before my adolescent eyes, a slender, beautifully proportioned body with an attractive bust and an alluring face . . . Which look, which mask should I pick? I've just got to get that body. Or else I'll never have a boyfriend, no one will ever love me, and life won't be worth living. The beauty factors are charm and love, the result is the meaning of life: that equation moves right into my brain (and a lot more deftly than $ax^2 + bx + c = 0$ ever did). The formula is written everywhere. In the novels serialized in my mother's newspapers. In the stories the bookstore owner recommends as suitable for a fourteen-year-old. The popular romance collections of Delly, Magali, and above all, the "My Daughter's Library" series with Elisabeth, Mme Bernage and her *Brigitte* books—all works with "high moral standards," and it isn't hard to figure out that this means the girls in these stories will get married without ever having made love beforehand. Still, they do lead enviable lives as pretty, polished young ladies: chaste, educated when necessary, often with their *baccalauréat*, but no profession afterward because they're supposed to get married. Nurses during wartime, of course. Girls living freely off on their own? There are some: black sheep who wear too much makeup, bad girls who pay for their loose ways with sorrow, remorse, illness, and poverty. I have a real fondness for those bohemian types, tough and adventurous, but obviously not heading in the right direction like Brigitte, who makes a fine marriage, is well-off, and winds up the happy mother of six. These antiseptic goody-goodies, I find, are always connected to the middle-class way of life, and if I feel that the good girls end up in better shape than the reckless ones, it's because they live in a shimmering dream of security and harmony. In the summertime, such women make jam in sprawling country houses with birdies twittering everywhere, while the ones who thought they could live just as they pleased are coughing and spitting off in a garret somewhere. I prefer happiness, naturally.

And then, in class, in the street, there are girls who saunter around with conceited expressions, fetching smiles; they make their skirts dance and pull their sweaters tight to show off their swelling breasts with a confidence that surprises me. And they're the ones who have a boyfriend waiting for them in a street near the school, who are all excited on Saturdays about the teen party that evening, who turn up on Monday with new slang picked up from the boys, "I really crammed for that math test but I flunked it anyway." Dreamers, too. I feel that they live life intensely.

"Zero, mademoiselle! You did not even open your geography book! Sometimes I wonder what goes on in your head!" Sly smiles from the friends in the know, curious looks from the others. And the unprepared student? Not one bit flustered, even proud, as though she were in possession of a secret compared to which the world's oil production is just so much kid stuff. Sitting down again with a superior air, she casually fluffs up her blond bangs with a forefinger. Supreme freedom. I admire girls in love before I join their ranks. What a sinking feeling when one of those privileged creatures leaves me with a "So long" when school lets out, crossing the street to join the boy who has just appeared on the opposite sidewalk. I go on home through a desert. Sometimes I meet Claudine, sashaying along on her high heels, a real vamp, terrifically cheap-looking, but trailing admirers. I can't help envying her. While I do my homework in the evening, I listen to the radio. "One day, you'll see, we'll meet and you'll belong to me . . ." I, too, will be chosen. But how? By throwing the whole business into gear. By energetically creating a seductive image for myself. With what servile diligence do I latch on to all the outward signs of the right femininity, the come-hither kind, and how tenaciously I try to prove I am a young woman at the age of fourteen. But as I see things at the time, those stockings, that straight skirt, those high heels aren't supposed to change me into a "sex object," but to make me happy by getting me chosen. Plus, when I can finally parade around with stockings and an appropriately busty sweater, I will have the impression of proclaiming my freedom. A bra? My dream. It doesn't occur to my mother to buy me such a thing; she is a country woman, and has never worn one. I don't dare mention it to her, because that would be an admission that I want my breasts to show, but what's the point of being "stacked" if it's not properly "packed": look for the Lou label wherever fine lingerie is sold. Luckily, a pal slips me one of her bras, and I am saved. My wish finally fulfilled. Girl talk in the recreation yard, and even later, in the *cité universitaire*: "Mine are a disaster, I'm sure she wears falsies, her boobs are so big she looks like a cow, you're as flat as a pancake, what you want is just enough to fill the hand of an honest man." A major concern. I admire myself in front of the mirror wearing those little cloth cups on my chest: front view, profile, shoulders back, arms raised. It's like a game. Yet men's remarks are already more or less accepted in advance. "What kind are you wearing, the white ones with lace are the sexiest, nice set you've got there." Why feel humiliated, they're just breasts like any others. Twisting and turning before the wardrobe mirror at fourteen, I am already reduced to my appearance in my own eyes; all that is missing is the gaze of the Other. In composition class in eighth grade, Marie-Thérèse likes to study herself in the dark reflection of the open window, running through a series of barely perceptible motions: she lifts her chin, lowers her head, thrusts out her breasts, pulling on her pendant at the same time to make them stand out. All those girls who can never get enough of looking at themselves, anywhere, in shop windows, between the pairs of shoes and the mannequins in their dresses, girls who always have a comb and mirror in their pockets. A quick pass with the comb, a pretext for checking your face while softly stroking your hair. In the girls' room, each one in front of her mirror, changing her mouth, her eyes. Obscene. I do it, too—hypnotize myself with my own reflection.

Brigitte, my bra-provider, says that she's too skinny, I'm a bit chubby and too tall, and men don't like tall women. She complains of being "obliged" to wear falsies. She has a habit of twisting her hair around a finger, and she smiles with her mouth closed because her teeth are crooked. Hard to do, given the hysterical laughter that comes over us out of the blue. We'd lost track of each other since the time of those instructive sessions in the bathroom; two years older than I am, she has quit school and is taking shorthand typing classes. We become friends because it's useful on Sundays: with two of us, we can go to the movies, to the motocross, or to the shop sales.

She is my instructor, because of the two years she has on me and because her entire small and determined self makes what she says so vivid that it seems indisputable. She arrives around two on a Sunday afternoon in a flutter of excitement. "So you're wearing your pleated skirt today," and then the critical appraisal, "It makes your legs look fat," followed by, "Did you notice, I washed my hair, it's all electric." Next we compare outfits, try on each other's things, a favorite pastime, and how do I look in this or that? One day when I've tied a cotton kerchief around my head, I await her verdict. A little smile and suddenly, in her affected movie-star voice, "You're a perfect wallflower." Annihilation in five seconds. But in her gloomy moments, she is equally hard on herself. "Beauties we're not, just standard issue." Not one square inch of flesh escapes her expert eye, not a single toe can wiggle freely, no legs are idly crossed. She's constantly calling me to order: "Hairy legs are ugly. You should wear polish on your toenails. You show too much thigh when you sit down." The body under constant surveillance and restraint, abruptly shattered into a heap of pieces—eyes, skin, hair—that must be dealt with one by one to reach perfection. Not an easy task, since a single detail can spoil everything: "Did you see that one, with her droopy butt!" Most of the time Brigitte is able to persuade me that she has a personal style, perhaps something along the lines of the actress Françoise Arnoul, attractive and mysterious, but definitely not too flashy. It's frightening how well she knows the code: be as cute and desirable as you like, but whatever you do, don't let anyone think you're "easy," one of her words. Unbeatable at detecting what looks "tarty"—a frizzy permanent, too bright a red, high heels with pants—or "country bumpkin": a slip showing, wearing green and yellow together. She skillfully avoids these twin perils. At her side I sometimes feel like a bloated eyesore, since my mother is still choosing my clothes and she's unaware of all these subtle distinctions. Even I am hard put to believe that black pants make you look cheap while the same ones in gray are fine. Looking back on all this, I now realize that Brigitte was trying not to look like a factory worker. An office job—that's different, and her dream is the simple, fresh, natural look that will land her a good catch: sober, hardworking, but preferably not working class. She would like to have love affairs (with the crooner Luis Mariano, she wouldn't hesitate), but they never work out. In the romance novels and photo-stories she lends me, the women are all treated like doormats, their lives are a shambles, and then wham: happiness. That doesn't work out for Brigitte, and I don't believe in it anymore. Her devotion to the idea of complete self-sacrifice doesn't suit me either; she says that when you love a man, you'll take anything from him, even eat his shit. Later I will hear other women, more cultured and refined, go on about passion, losing oneself in the Other and so on, but it's basically the same thing.

I start using Brigitte's strange words. I've already seen them often in print, but hearing them in her mouth proves to me that one can use this language in real life. She talks about seducers and femmes fatales, about sensual mouths. Her other main interests intrigue me as well. She cuts out photos of film

stars like Daniel Gélin and Gérard Philipe from *Cinémonde*. So
do I. She can tell you all the new songs, and her secret desire is
to go on a radio talent contest and be discovered, but she never
dares or maybe isn't sure she'd win. I envy her ability to take
down a song like "*C'est magnifique*" in shorthand. Five o'clock
on a Sunday afternoon: two girls stagger out of the movie theater on place des Belges. The world is a shimmer of gray; people's heads look tiny and ugly. The girls drift through the crowd
slowly flowing along the shopping streets. Tentative pauses
before the dresses and magazines. Gérard Philipe and Michèle
Morgan continue to run toward each other across burning
Mexican sands. Some guys are following us. Don't answer,
they'll think you're encouraging them. Brigitte is teaching me
the ropes, running through the rules over and over again. Look
good to everybody but don't let just anyone come up to you.
Especially if they're guys "from the boonies." We get tired of
strolling in front of the same windows. No one interesting.
Then we move on to the streets without stores, sometimes
going as far as the edge of the forest. The primroses may be
blossoming by the side of the road and the pussy willows bursting into bloom in the woods at the end of March, but with
Brigitte I'm never off on a voyage of discovery. As far as she's
concerned, nature is where you get some fresh air after you've
been cooped up in an office all week. Even stargazing is turned
to good use: if you count nine of them for nine days running,

then you'll dream of the man you'll marry. I go along without protest on these truncated walks. We talk about songs, movie stars, boys. No. More than that.

Brigitte often lets herself go, forgetting the tame sentimentality of *Nous Deux*, and her proper-young-lady pose falls by the wayside. Together, we talk about "it." And girls, I know, are not supposed to talk about "it." Endlessly informative, she is, and she sets me free every Sunday with her jokes and raw language. With her, the world is one big sex organ, a colossal itch, a flood of sperm and blood. She knows everything, that men go with men and women with women, what you have to do so you won't have a kid. Incredulous, I rummage through the night table. Nothing. Underneath the mattress I find a rumpled napkin, stiffened by stains. A horrible object. A real sacrilege. What word does she say, the one men use, "come," "cream," we wouldn't know them yet, maybe the scientific term, perhaps she read it somewhere, sperm, but what is writing it compared to hearing it out loud in your parents' bedroom when you're thirteen years old? We tell each other stuff that would have appalled our elders. Anything at all can become obscene. Legs waving in the air, organs gaping or erect, the banality of porn rags—our stories are better, and more cheerful, too. No discrimination: our conversations, whether technical or just for laughs, give equal time to both sexes. Impossible to feel ashamed with Brigitte on the day I feel that first shudder under the sheets—that happens to me, too, she laughs, but don't go telling the priest, it's none of his business.

And what a triumph when I announce to her that I have "it" now, too—no more pretending to have monthly cramps for me! I'm perfectly comfortable with my new condition.

No, I hadn't imagined it like this: casually lifting my pleated skirt, pulling down my panties and sitting on the toilet seat, not thinking of anything in particular, the elastic tight around my thighs just over the knees. Utter astonishment. Seeing what I've never seen before, my own blood, that blood. A part of my life is over. I sit staring the way fortune-tellers study tea leaves. That's it. Five minutes later my mother is joking awkwardly, "Now you've become a young woman." Neither more nor less of a young woman than I was the day before. It's simply a marvelous event. Impossible to tell my mother how pleased I am— Brigitte is the only one who will understand that. I'm already going over the story in my head: So there I was, off to school on Monday as usual . . . And planning to mention to her as well my fear that it will suddenly stop, and the fact that while I would have liked a nice, limpid stream, I've got a swampy dribble, and what's hers like?

It seems I can talk to her about anything. Surely it's this frank language that binds me to her, and that will later make me feel ashamed. No pruderies as at school, nothing you can't confess. "Me, I like looking at women's bosoms in the movies!" I can still hear her confident tone, on those summer Sundays, as she nibbles on the grass blades she keeps plucking and spitting out: "Women don't enjoy doing it, my mother told me." Then those cat's-eyes of hers, and her laugh: "Too bad, I'm going to enjoy it!" I like the talk about our bodies and the laughter, above all. But I'm sure that it's wrong. The ideal: that other Brigitte, the one in the series of books for girls, who goes to art shows and never says a dirty word. My Brigitte, she doesn't forget that either, the code of the real young lady. "I'm going to enjoy it!" But she gets up, gracefully smoothes out her dress, and puts on a dignified expression, nose in the air. All our talk is kept just between us, so that other people won't take us for depraved sluts who've "been around." The code is even built into our secret conversations. I learn everything there is to know about virginity from Brigitte, and no mistake: the painful opening of this door by a man, breaking a seal of good conduct whose absence is impossible to hide, except with shots of astringent lemon, which aren't a sure thing anyway. After Mass one day, Renée, Brigitte's friend from the office, throws her head back and half-closes her eyes, saying rapturously, "He told me, if you're not a virgin on our wedding night, you hear me, I'll strangle you!" We're in front of the electric household appliance and luggage store. What a thrill. As for unwed mothers, tough luck. Men can screw around as much as they want, in fact it's actually better for them to have experience so they can "initiate" us. In spite of my active childhood and natural curiosity, I simply accept the idea of being offered up on my back. I don't find this passivity disgusting to imagine: dreaming of a big bed or looking up at the sky from a grassy couch, a face bending over me . . . The rest of the process is always in his hands, never mine. I admit, we dare to describe our periods and our longings, but marriage begins to seem obligatory and sacred with Brigitte. And although we talk about our sexuality, it is tacitly understood that we cannot imagine being able to go all the way with it.

Not easy to determine the respective effects of conditioning and freedom: I thought the line my girlhood followed was a straight one, but it goes off in all directions. One thing is certain, my Brigitte period proves calamitous for my mother, whose glorious image takes some rude knocks. The damage is petty, but telling: dusty furniture, unmade beds, a spreading waistline. On my own home ground, Brigitte makes me see what I had hitherto felt without attaching any importance to it. No, my mother doesn't know how to cook, not even to make mayonnaise, housework doesn't interest her, and she isn't "feminine." That terrible pronouncement, one day during an argument: "Your mother's a cow." Most of the time it isn't that direct, more of a laughing matter and lots of "you knows": "You know, your hairbrush could use a good soak! You've never heard of ammonia? Ver-y use-ful." The economic approach: "My mother makes my dresses, all of them, it's much less expensive that way." I always reply that my mother hasn't the time, which is true, but why make that excuse and be ashamed to say that she'd rather see to her business and calculate her profit margins? Why be ashamed to admit she wouldn't know how to sew a dress for me? Worst of all, Brigitte's prying eyes the first time she found my father mashing the potatoes—oh, what an extraordinary sight—and the horrible astonishment of her pointed question: "You're the one who does that?" Strange animals in a zoo, from another planet. You're the one who peels the potatoes! You're the one who does the dishes! Other girl-friends later on will show their amazement less blatantly, perhaps, but I can feel it all the same. Your father's the one who—what a weird aberration, what a joke, like the guy in the *Paris Match* cartoons, the one wearing the frilly apron. If only my mother had some attenuating circumstances, fragile health or a horde of brats, but no. As though they have deliberately chosen to live in an abnormal fashion. I fail to persuade Brigitte that this way of doing things is unimportant, and even rather practical for the business. A househusband, unbelievable. And suddenly they're both ridiculous: my gentle father is now a Milquetoast, and my mother, with all her vitality, is wearing the pants in the family. Now I am ashamed that he puts up with doing the dishes, that she shouts like that. And how I cherish the image of an industrious but discreet mother—a little Dresden china figurine, what a dream—instead of that powerful explosion. They're so awkward, the both of them, they don't fit the pattern. Which pattern? The one you see in nice, decent families, or families that are trying to be that way. It's not proper for a man to be peeling vegetables; he ought to be a bit like the others, interested in sports, yelling at the slightest bad grade, grounding the culprit, sending slaps flying right and left. At school, these blustering fathers are a big success, and some girls proudly recount the latest paternal exploits: he locked me in my room, no parties until Easter. He's their enemy, but they seem to adore him. Maternal authority doesn't go over as well, however—too much hidden resentment involved. To top it off we get *Les Femmes savantes* in ninth grade, and we're obliged to find those "learned ladies" comical (it's Molière, after all), to dump on Philaminthe and applaud Chrysale in her big monologue, even though I secretly don't think it's very funny.

Brigitte's house is a shining example of normality for me. Mme Desfontaines, always there, busy-busy in her kitchen, a little washing, a little sewing, dainty chores, and don't go into the dining room, you'll get it dirty. A tiny universe, to my eyes, preoccupied with trivial tasks, like polishing the doorknobs, what a joke, and how can anyone seriously spend five minutes wondering whether to make noodles or shepherd's pie? A universe in slow motion, impressively quiet to someone who lives day in and day out in the crucible of voices I call home. The silence of those kitchens in the afternoon. Empty, oppressive, not like the silence in school when the students are working, that full silence ready to explode into shouting and laughter outside. A numbing silence. I can't wait to leave. That's where I discover an astonishing and unexpected domestic complicity between mother and daughter. "Did you see your sweater? I washed it in soap flakes—like new. I'm going to make you a new bedspread: cretonne would be nice, I think," and so on. Brigitte helps out in the kitchen and smugly makes me feel that I don't know how to do a thing. It's true, I can't whip up a mayonnaise or even peel a carrot efficiently, but I could say that in school I manage rather well. No, that won't make up for it. Everyone understands that for a girl, not knowing how to do a thing means being incapable of cooking, cleaning, ironing properly. How will you cope later on when you're married? The big question, with its irrefutable logic, to rub your nose right in it, can't even boil an egg, well just wait, you'll see how your husband likes eating out of cans! Makes me giggle—marriage is so far off, and I watch absentmindedly as Brigitte pulls her sheets taut, smoothing every wrinkle from the bed, instead of drawing the covers up like I do. All the same, I start to think there must be "something missing." Since all girls and women have to look after their homes, I should learn those things too, as well as my future profession. One summer during my adolescence, despite my mother's shrugs—don't waste your time with that, go ride your bike—I clean my room every morning, and even hers, too, since I am now so easily offended by messiness. I iron dishcloths, handkerchiefs, simple things, to get into the habit. I hang up the wash: a towel, a clothespin; a shirt, a clothespin; slowly festooning the line as the mild September breeze caresses my legs. Girls' work, quiet and innocent. On Sundays, I make chocolate mousse. Proudly. I can do it, too. At the family dinner on August 15, Ascension Day, I bask in the attention; they all dig in, happily stuffing themselves with my chocolate mousse, saying, "Much better than store-bought!" No more, "What's to become of that one!" The exultation of being complete, with nothing missing anymore. But I shouldn't make too much of this ironing and baking; it's fun, a game, a relaxing change from reading, a way to stave off boredom toward the end of vacation, an excuse to taste with impunity the provoking sweetness of eggs and sugar beaten together, to eat whole spoonfuls of warm melted chocolate. As soon as school starts again, that's the end of domestic diversions. First things first.

My mother, the teachers, that's what they all tell me. I believe them, but the future is clouding over. Primary school teacher will be fine. Bad enough that people say, "Teachers don't get married." School becomes a drag: I'm into a serious slump. After I hit the eighth grade, nothing really interests me anymore in class. The Chasles formula or Euclid's postulate, pretend that you have lost something dear to you in 250 words or more, well, I couldn't care less. The French Revolution, Hiroshima, a few *explications de texte*—perhaps a flicker of interest. As far as work is concerned, I've outlived my former enthusiasm: my eager curiosity is all gone, leaving only a fierce desire not to fail, sheer pride and nothing more. Or else I don't dare bank entirely on my charm, keeping two irons in the fire, whatever the cost. I prefer to think that I'm not completely shucking off a certain idea of myself: if I do nothing, I am nothing—my mother's words. But what energy it takes, during those desperate years, not to lose ground. Evenings when I spend three hours cranking out my geometry homework, tracing straight lines and perpendiculars with a song by Aznavour running through my head. In class I slouch in my chair, elbows on the desk, face propped up in my hands, eyes seemingly riveted on the book or the blackboard. The perfect position for daydreaming. I develop the habit of switching off the teacher after the first few words; for four years I never listen to one lesson from start to finish, and try to catch up in the evenings with my textbooks. Some teachers dictate the lessons, which is more tiring, but with a bit of practice you can manage to write while thinking of something else: boys, fantasies of romance, songs, longings . . . Yes, I heartily recommend the seated position. I'm wrapped in a big soft dream from which I emerge painfully to translate a Latin passage. As we walk home from the movies on Sunday, when I think of the homework awaiting me—while Brigitte trots along at my side toward her cozy evening of getting her clothes ready for Monday, washing her hair to look nice for the accountant—sometimes, just for a moment, I envy that placid, carefree existence. What will we be quizzed on tomorrow, and what about all those things I still have to learn, those pages to write, those exams to pass? How about a little job, typing's pleasant enough; you'd have money to buy clothes and could go out whenever you want, like most girls, a life of pure futility, and waiting . . . My parents' acquaintances and customers are starting to make knowing remarks. "Well, your girl's going to be leaving you one of these days soon, heh heh!" My mother gets a mite testy. "She's got plenty of time, let her enjoy her youth," but sometimes she adds, "Marriage is part of life," and says she'd hate to see me left an old maid. These days, I long to take it easy, not be so responsible, and I tell myself that studying is a practical way to spend the meantime, because after all, you have to go on living while you wait for your grand passion. Letting someone take your hand, *mon enfant ma soeur*, Baudelaire's invitation to a voyage of love . . . The gleaming kitchen, the strawberries under a musical stream of water, one day, you'll see, we'll meet and you'll belong to me. And nothing in school to successfully counteract this confused obligation to please, to be loved, to be chosen. The good sisters rant about "modesty," fulminate against wearing pants that arouse men's desire (another reason to wear them) and urge us to read *Christiane*, a magazine with photographs of girls in the most incredibly dowdy outfits, wearing idiotic smiles of beatific Christian joy, who wax ecstatic about the upright life and pure, honest friendship with boys. The sisters pass around *Now That You've Become a Woman*, a set of instructions for body and soul that reeks of restriction and boredom. Nothing but pitfalls to be avoided, in delicately veiled terms, and above all, watch out for boys, as they are "physically very different from you in their reactions," the victims of "a sudden, imperious impulse that they cannot control." Whereas we, it seems, don't feel all that much, so if we give in, it's on purpose—a fine distinction. To this advice for perfect innocents, our favorite insult between us girls, I prefer the novels and tips on how to have a blooming complexion in *Echo de la mode*, a popular women's weekly. The only religion that makes my heart beat faster at the age of fifteen is love. I'll do anything, if you ask me—Piaf is right. And I wake up for Corneille's *Le Cid*, love and honor, preposterous, but in any case preferable to the War of the Austrian Succession. Are my classmates all off in dreamland the way I am? I remember their "I sure slept through that!" in French, in math. All apparently diligent, homework always done, never any rebellion, nothing but chuckles and whispering. We just want to get by, a herd with no ambition. There are exceptions: Leguet, the workaholic, one of the few we all know will go far, but forget admiration—what a weirdo, sullen, dressed any old how, and so we rather pity her instead of envying her brains. After the big push at the end of ninth grade, complete collapse in the tenth. Our math teacher is an enormous woman who wears a black cloak over her checked blouse. She's a screamer. "Mesdemoiselles, you are not putting your hearts into it! Nothing but numbskulls and lazy lumps! A little enthusiasm if you please!" Pure Greek. As the years go by, the faces in the classroom change. Some weeding out. First the ones without much money, off to be secretaries or salesclerks, then the shopkeepers' daughters, also in the selling line but with a different air, and the farm girls who vanish forever into their acres. Others arrive; the convent school is full of shooting stars: scatterbrained things expelled from *lycées*, languid lovelies who get married during the next school holiday, airheads forever off in the clouds, and always a tyrannical father thrown in for good measure. Children of people of means, girls who care only for dancing, partying, and listening to the moody songs of Brassens. I soon fall under their influence. Replacing the picture of Jean Marais in my math notebook with one of James Dean seems like an improvement to me, as does switching from Mariano to the Platters, never realizing that it's still the same crush. Discussing the future with my new friends means talking about flirting, the same as with Brigitte. Pop stars, boyfriends, clothes, and gossip about one another are the main topics of our conversations. I feel I've come a long way.

Now we hit the bumpy part of the story, telling my good fortune, la-dee-da, except it isn't that good, more like a drubbing that leads to humiliation and revolt. I head toward boys the way one sets out on a journey. With fear and curiosity. I don't know what they're like. The last time I looked, they were throwing chestnuts at me on street corners in the summer, and snowballs outside the school gate in the winter. Or shouting insults at us from the opposite sidewalk with me calling them jerks or assholes, depending on the circumstances, namely whether there were any adults around or not. Restless, manic creatures, a bit silly. It has taken a whole blessed afternoon of roller-skating to transfigure one of them. They have probably changed as much as I have. I set off in their direction, lightly equipped with advice gleaned from girl talk, *Echo de la mode*, novels, songs, a few poems of Musset and an overdose of dreams. Bovary's little sister. And deep down inside, hidden away as indecent, the desire for a pleasure I've discovered on my own. This other half of the world is a mystery to me, true, but I am sure I'm going to enjoy the party. The idea of any inequality between boys and myself, of any difference beyond the physical ones, simply never occurs to me because I've never experienced such a distinction. What a disaster.

The party never gets going. A strapping girl, dressed okay but hardly fetchingly, her straight hair ritually permanented each May ever since her First Communion—in men's language we're talking "dog." Lots of girls know "instinctively" how to make themselves attractive. Not me. One day, in despair, I spit at my face in the mirror. Sunday afternoons get more and more grim, and there is Brigitte, always so leery of being approached. It takes me a long time to figure out she is looking for the *real thing*, she is dying to make love, but only after getting married. Always turning her nose up at our Sunday followers, but then I'm not interested in them, either. "Hey girlies, haven't we met somewhere before?"The admiration of zeroes—that's twice nothing. I ignore them with no trouble, quite as unfairly as the guys I'm sure I'd like are ignoring me. But how and where to meet them? Brigitte has just one male coworker in her office and he's "going steady" with a hairdresser. The only girls who would invite me to their parties are the daughters of dentists, wholesalers, and foundry engineers, my former goody-goody classmates, and they aren't my friends. There's not much mixing in a little town of eight thousand inhabitants. The public dance on Saturday nights, you're kidding, nothing but housemaids and factory girls. Why don't I have a brother—he'd take me out, he'd have friends; all those girls constantly talking about their brothers, he just got his *baccalauréat*, he's home on leave, he says that motor scooters are kid stuff. The brother-god. Too bad for me. Sometimes the trip isn't an easy one. Which leaves luck, and there's not a whole lot of that around.

As pickups go, it's a good one. He says his lines perfectly, perhaps just a bit too quickly. Tall, tanned like a model in an Ambre Solaire ad, a warm voice with a pleasant timbre, like a soap opera star's. He says something complicated, adding, "That's from Racine, I think." I can't tell if he's putting us on because the only Racinian play I've read is *Les Plaideurs*. Brigitte is flipping through her magazines and I'm eating peaches at the edge of a field right outside town. The Racine part is just before he lays his Vespa at the side of the gravel road and comes over to sit down casually, wrapping his arms around his knees, playing with his dark glasses and speaking in a relaxed manner. Well-phrased things, not like that haven't-I-seen-you-someplace-before bunk, quite nicely done. Just like a movie, without the music. And yet it's horrible. I have never been so upset, my hands are trembling as I try to peel my peach, dribbling juice all down my wrist. Panicky embarrassment. Alone, I would have bolted. I hate him for talking and because we really don't know what to reply, aside from yes, no, it depends, fourteen, ninth grade, Gérard Philipe, Bécaud's my favorite singer. He's studying us from behind his sunglasses. Brigitte is sucking on her grass blade and periodically emitting little bleating laughs. He's wearing shorts, no shirt; I can see his muscles, his skin. Good-looking. It's scary. That's when I leave childhood behind, in the shame of that gaze directed half at me, half at my friend, that all-purpose sweet talk intended for either one of us at the same time. I could stop here, pretend that the game horrifies me. Not true, since I stay right where I am. After all, it's wonderful to be watched from behind dark glasses. He leans over to look at Brigitte's magazines, looking up at each of us in turn. "You ought to wear your hair like this." He shows me a girl on the cover of *Nous Deux*. "And you, Brigitte, like this." He doesn't tell us we're cute—even better, he implies it. What's the expression, "to tame." Frightened young things, wary little kittens, the nice tanned boy isn't going to hurt you. It's probably normal for men to talk to girls this way. I grow tame. Slowly I persuade myself that this chance meeting resembles an Adventure. An interesting guy, twenty-three, a chemist, he says. I even dare ask him where he lives. Despite his skillful patter, however, our vacation pickup artist is unable to pry apart the Siamese twins we form out of fear, even more out of jealousy, so that he can take us for a ride on the Vespa, each in turn. "*Ciao*," he tells us, "see you tomorrow!" *Ciao*, a new word. We're impressed.

Then, for the first time, I indulge in that strange conversation about boys and feelings, the circular conversation you keep thinking will clear everything up, an interminable commentary in which you become all bogged down. Did you hear, he's a chemist. Did you hear, he's twenty-three, I didn't think he was that old. Me neither. Laughter, you could see the hair on his stomach; laughter again, there's more where that came from. We can't save ourselves with obscenity. A really neat guy, he must have all the girls he wants. Flattered that he chose us, when there's so much better around. The murmurs of slaves, incense offered to the god. Just talking about him I'm falling in love. I make resolutions for the following day: I shouldn't be so aggressive, it must have put him off a bit. We debate who should take the first ride on the Vespa. Brigitte hums "*Mes mains dessinent dans le soir, la forme d'un espoir.*" Hope springs eternal . . . Our bikes are leaning against the embankment where we left them three hours earlier. What an adventure. Later on, when I'm twenty, I watch Molière's Don Juan up on stage, putting the moves on Mathurine and Charlotte each in turn; it's fascinating, and I feel sick. We weren't that silly and provincial. That taken in, yes.

The next day, I put my hair in a ponytail like the one on the cover of *Intimité*. Even though we go back the following days as well, until Brigitte's vacation is over, he never shows up again. Sometimes we tell ourselves he had to return unexpectedly to Le Havre, and sometimes we decide he thought we were mousy or prissy. Too late. Not one iota of revolt or contempt. We aren't angry at him. Submissiveness in all its perfection at fourteen years old. Later on, I take that ride on the Vespa a hundred times, between the Defenestration of Prague and verbs that take the subjunctive. My first adventure, somewhat revised (in particular by consigning Brigitte to oblivion), becomes one more of the many love stories with which we all while away the time in class. Now I can say it, a lousy creep who couldn't manage to chalk up two morons, but that's not how I think of it at the time. Gérard I love you, that's how I write it up on my scratch pad, and in my head, "my first love." It's the only language I know.

Actually, he doesn't make it past Christmas. I think he's old, at twenty-three, an inequality I do notice, and easily find repulsive. And I have hopes of meeting other Vespas. "What will happen to me?" There it is, the one and only big question, my entire metaphysics until the age of seventeen. Leaving school after class, nose to the wind, wearing a fashionably baggy coat, a hard-won "look" that makes me seem like a big gawk of a girl, but too bad. O this fragile victory, my appearance: a trifle—a look, a remark—is enough to demolish me. And they're past masters of the deflating pin prick, Brigitte and my classmates, but they're not the ones I have to please. It's over, Mother, I can't hear you anymore. Listen to my high, thin little voice: it doesn't sound like yours. You drive me crazy by missing the point when I tell you Françoise is going out with So-and-so, that Marie-Jo goes to parties every Saturday. I harp on the freedom of others in hopes of cadging a bit for my own personal use. Nothing doing, blind to comparisons, "Luckily you're not like them." But I am. At sixteen I no longer recognize the upright and determined image of myself you throw in my face.

Relaxed, small-town pickups, more like impromptu palling around: either you know each other or you will one day, never any rough stuff. Strolling along, watched by the same old ladies at their windows and the same shopkeepers standing in their doors, we feel spied on but protected. A far cry from the big city prowled by tomcats of sex and crime. Who's picking up whom, I'm not too clear on the difference at this point. Like many other girls, I "do the roundabout," passing and repassing in front of the stores, while boys pass and repass as well, sized up out of the corners of our eyes, the not-too-bads and the god-awfuls. We loiter. Office workers, students at a business school, a few from the *lycées* of Rouen on Saturdays and Sundays. They're a late discovery for me, boys my own age. At first I find them funny, more or less amusing, with their puns and spoonerisms, so sure that we girls can't do that, really witty, how did I manage to live without "I thought it was an oyster but it's not." I'm not forearmed by a bourgeois-intellectual education against the nastier wordplay and I haven't got the proper young lady's oh-my-virgin-ears reflex of wrinkling my nose at vulgar allusions. Of course I laugh. But I must soon admit, it's always the same tired jokes—she's a carpenter's dream, flat as a board—and I've already heard the dirty stories from Brigitte. The boys seem almost as wild and ridiculous as they did in their snowball period. And surprise: always talking about themselves, their likes and dislikes, their classes, their detentions, their motor scooters, and their balls. Listening to men, paying attention to them—now it starts. You can let them talk, or you can laugh. Unless you choose to play dumb, saying silly things on purpose to crack them up. "She's sweet," they laugh, mocking and conceited. And always dragging us into their universe: come bowling, play some pool, I've a race, a match today, yes, yes I'll come watch you. They never imagine we might also have our own world, interests, school, girlfriends, but that's enough of that, you know those nuns of yours are all old dykes, period. When I feel like talking about the difficulties of advanced math, about my favorite writers, Rousseau for example, they're annoyed, and girls' algebra problems are nothing compared to theirs. At home, at my school, girls have always been encouraged to study hard, but with them such success is a drawback, makes them suspicious, another pain in the ass, bookworms turn them off, they like their girls unspoiled, with no complexes. They make fun of me when I want to go home and study. I must get used to the idea that for a long time, no boy, no man, except my father, will attach any importance to what I do. Teacher? Up shoot the eyebrows. Lawyer? You'll get swollen ankles from being on your feet all day. Some of them are repelled—that nice blond guy, so kind and loving: but honey, I'm afraid all this studying will wear you out, why don't you find a job as a secretary? Having brains must be what means you're not a real woman anymore to them. One day I'm with some boys and we run into Leguet, the top student in my school; when I say hello, the others start hooting and choking with laughter. "What a ghastly sight! Who is that horror?" She's incredibly smart, I protest, because I do envy her a little, deep down, in spite of my timidity. But I'd rather die than hear people talk about me the way they do behind her back, and I can't even imagine giving up the things she sacrifices. Admiring glances, my vague hopes for the future, love, intimacy, the Other . . .

There it is already, the awful mess I won't be able to escape. I need boys, but to please them I'd have to be simperingly sweet, admit that they're always right, use "feminine wiles." Kill what still resists, the love of accomplishment, the desire to be really truly myself. That or loneliness. That or looking at my lips and breasts and telling myself they're useless. That, obviously. But I don't go about it the right way. I sneer aggressively at their boasting. I try stubbornly to talk about what I love, books, poetry, oh enough they say, stuff it—why, when I can put up with the talk about soccer and inoculations against hoof-and-mouth disease (a vet school student) and the ritual jokes about comparing penis sizes in the shower at the *lycée*? Just a minute, my girl, not the same thing at all, listen carefully, prick up your ears, ha ha! You mustn't be a pain around boys, don't you know that? What I don't know is how to hide from a boy that I like him. Men want to do the choosing, sweetheart. So what, I like to choose too, I still don't understand the difference. This blunder—switching roles—immediately gets you labeled a pushover: she's easy. No such thing as an easy boy. One day I'm out there cruising happily, without thinking about it; I pass in front of the business school, he should be getting out now . . . Not there. Never one to stand around, where is he, rue du Nord, the roundabout, I'm off and running. A bunch of them, then a voice, like a punch in the face: "Her again!" The dirty creep. I storm off with my book-bag, seething with rage. I don't know how to behave, I'm either too much or not enough, standoffish and boy-crazy at the same time, a dizzy smile, breathless with admiration, and then tired of the role I have to play. I don't want that ride on the scooter any-more. I feel it's all my fault. "Boys will be boys," it says in my English grammar book. An example of a universal truth.

That trip, what am I waiting for . . . If I'd listened to myself, I think I'd still be there waiting. True love would be so wonderful. But all around me in class, and Brigitte, too, they "know." While I don't. The best way to get it

over with—just calmly choose a partner. He's on line with me
at the post office; furtive glances, harmless conversation, kept
up until the roundabout. Boring, and his thick mouth, his math-
student look—good grades, but not one of the top stars—don't
say anything to me. He'll be the one. Trot out the smiles, friendly expressions, fine, see you Monday. No, really, it's not bad,
even if it isn't like a scene from a novel, even if I am tossing all
the tender preliminaries out the window. Why always drench
things in syrup, carve two hearts on a tree trunk to guarantee a
fond memory? Three days of waiting, windy days in late March,
like a three-day retreat before First Communion, the same
slowness, the same torpor. I prepare myself, and my head a lot
more than my body. I go over everything in my imagination, figure out how much time I have, because my mother keeps a close
watch on me. My navy blue sweater, the white collar, my bangs
combed, I'm ready an hour early. Liberation, ceremony or sacrifice, who knows. I can still feel how determined I was, strid-
ing off to the traffic circle. What's going to happen to me?
Whatever it is, I'm the one making it happen. When I see him
coming toward me in a duffel coat, wearing a big smile, I'd like
to run away. You take the rough with the smooth, and I'm the
one who started this. Limp phrases, our steps echoing on the
deserted sidewalks; it's Monday, so three-quarters of the shops
are closed. The poster from Sunday's film is still up: *Les Jeunes
Années d'une reine*, with Romy Schneider. Quietly boring. Not so

much freedom after all, I'm not in charge; at most I'm allowed to suggest, "Why don't we take that street?" He gives me a funny look, quick put on the ditzy act, "I just love daffodils, the gardens over that way are full of them, come on!" First the arm around the shoulders, heavy, terrible. The voice, suddenly lower and softer. Aha. Here it comes. The opposite sex has scratchy cheeks, a hard body, and breathes heavily. Touched neither by the grace of pleasure nor the blessing of a great emotion, I am somewhat surprised. There is no sunshine, and I don't feel at all as though I were in a dream. It's more like the acute consciousness that follows a night of insomnia, when you can see and hear everything but just can't find the right words. An old woman chatting over a gate with her neighbor looks over at us and remarks, "Everyone has their springtime, that's how it goes." He's holding me too tightly, I feel like a fool walking along stiff-legged, stopping every ten yards. I'm thinking of the *baccalauréat* exams, and the coming summer. I've moved on to the next stage; one of my questions has been answered. I trot home happily. "You were at the dentist's a long time!" "Yes, the office was crowded." My mother looks at me from behind her counter. Today I'm paying her back for her silence about nooky and everything else. I go up to my room, thinking about what the other girls have told me: "I washed myself right after, I absolutely had to, and my heart was beating like wild." Me, I look at myself in the mirror, wondering why I feel just the same.

So far, so good; I'm eager to continue the trip. A single encounter and the swift revelation of a complicity that has never ceased to move me. There hadn't been the slightest flicker of triumph in his eyes—there, I got you—or else I haven't yet learned to recognize it. I'd seen only a boy who didn't talk much, a face already like a brother's. Over the next few months we spend about forty hours together; I keep track, as though I were adding to a hoard of special moments. The sun warms my face but the earth is still cool beneath my back. During my walks in the country with my mother, I'd often caught sight, at a distance, of shapes with blurred outlines. Couples. I hadn't been able to take my eyes off them—whatever were they up to? And here I am in turn. Amazing. I'm living the great dream of my childhood, the scenes of kissing and embracing so often imagined and acted out. Where is the guilt I thought I would feel—and the love? The idea that going out with a boy is some kind of pinnacle of experience is definitely dead, almost laughable. Our two bookbags lie side by side in the grass, but a life together, forget it. For the first time I'm terrorized by the idea of marriage. I'm beginning to emerge, to disencumber myself. Enough of this true-romance foolishness, the love-of-my-life stuff. There'll be other guys besides Rémi. I tackle my classwork with a blunt new energy; I need to pass the first part of the *baccalauréat* so that next year in twelfth grade I can seek the answers to questions that have been bothering me ever since I began finding this business of love and men

less complicated than I'd thought. I read. Sartre, Camus, naturally. How frivolous my problems with clothes and bad dates now
seem. Liberating texts that release me forever from serial stories
and women's novels. I ignore the fact that these books were written by men, that their heroes are men as well: Roquentin or
Meursault, I identify with them. What do you do with your life?
The question has no sex, neither does the answer, and this I
naively believe, that year of my bac. I have one motto: don't ever
do anything you'll regret. Where did I pick up that maxim? I'm
not reading Gide yet, and it never occurs to me that this ambition is impracticable for a girl. But it soon will. Going out with
my parents or Rémi: which would I regret not doing? Easy, so
find some pretext, lie nonstop, and bingo! I'm off. Yes but what
do I do with this desire that arrives along with summer skirts and
the heavy petting sanctioned by two months of dating? I always
want to go further. So does he. His hand fumbles behind my back
for the first time, a stunning development; I hold my breath, and
hear the faint click as the strap is unhooked. But as in those novels I no longer read, "I push him violently away." Because they
come flooding back in on me, all those cautionary precepts for
girls, and sweep away my principles of freedom: "No one
respects girls who go too far," "Once you start you can't stop,"
the slippery slope, the downward path so luridly described in
Confidences. And what if I end up like Marine, whom all the boys
call One Size Fits All? When her ponytail flashes on the corner of

place des Belges, they all cackle, here comes the Doormat! And
the girls giggle too. For years I never hear anyone defend the sexual liberty of girls, and certainly not the girls themselves. Marine
has slept with at least three guys, so she's a slut. I worry: am I
maybe a bit sluttish around the edges, as they put it? Liberty, slut-
tery. I don't feel strong enough to choose to be a tart. And then
the rhythm method, some fine figuring, infallible, we've all got it
neatly copied in a notebook, but I don't believe that little calendar can tame the mute, invisible thing, as though the uterus and
ovaries didn't exist, but they're always waiting, like a baby bird's
beak. Impossible to gauge precisely the strength of this fear. All
those Greek and Racinian tragedies, they're in my womb. Fate in
all its absurdity. One sunny day, your life is over in one fell
swoop: the bridal veil or a small suitcase and the kid, a miserable
fix. Compared to that, Camus's revolt and philosophical aspira-
tions to freedom don't amount to squat. I'm fond of my silent
companion; we have good times, sometimes, and I'm dying to
make love with him. No. I don't feel like having my future grind
to a halt on the twenty-eighth of each month. I'll never be closer than I am at seventeen to sexual freedom and a glorious sen-
suality. And I discover immediately that they are out of reach.
This first, clearly perceived difference drives me to despair—I
feel it will never be abolished. Boys are free to desire, not you my
girl, resist, that's the code. Resistance methods? The usual defen-
sive game of dividing my body into territories from head to toe:

permitted area; the uncertain field of current maneuvers; the
forbidden zone. Cede territory only inch by inch. Each pleasure
is labeled defeat for me, victory for him. I had not anticipated
experiencing the discovery of the Other in terms of loss, and it
isn't amusing. My girlfriends and I reveal our "cowardice" with
shame, never with pleasure or pride. I prefer to be alone again.

Saved. My girlhood is marked by magic words that help me
to live, summing up events in a kind of ethics in action. Saved.
Not so much my virginity, that mute and tiresome scrap of skin;
I have never managed to persuade myself that it's worthwhile. At
most, it's useful, the last parry, a mealymouthed argument for
refusal: no thanks, I'm a virgin. But I rediscover the happiness of
walking really and truly alone through the streets, looking at
other men without feeling guilty, laughing heartily in class
instead of whispering secrets and passing notes under the desks,
all that sentimental mush that girls indulge in over boys. Weeks
stretch out ahead of me, clear of routine dates. Saved from a
dependence that had been settling in without my noticing it. I
want new things, to pass my *bac* exam and escape the good sisters to spend my senior year at the *lycée*, a year I know will be a
revelation—I can't let religion wreck it for me. And I long for
the big city, too, for anonymous streets lined with tall old houses:
Rouen, the reward-city of my childhood, the festive city, will
finally become my everyday city. I will leave the small-business
life behind, the omnipresent smell of coffee that seems to have

soaked into the very walls, the voices chanting about the weather, the cost of living, and death. Am I strong enough? My father says nothing; my mother thinks it over and exclaims, "Leave if you want to—a girl's not meant to be tied forever to her mother's apron strings!"

I pass my *bac* and prepare to move to a room in the girls' hostel in Rouen. Brigitte has gotten married. There they are, the both of them, sitting next to each other at a table in the café, paying me a visit after their honeymoon. I don't know what to say to them, as though there were no longer anything in common between a couple and a single girl. What should we talk about, anyway, when our former conversations were devoted to love and boys? Now that she's taken care of in that department, she can just sit there and smile. I watch her beaming excitedly, we've found an apartment, I'll keep working for a while until we've got our furniture. So many cockeyed plans, so many songs crooned by Mariano, so many dreams—to end up with this guy, who looks so clumsy sitting next to her, and who replies, to my what-are-you-having, with "a glass of umbrella juice." It's just not fair. The first one of us to betray—I don't know what, exactly: the hopes of our childhood, our taste for adventure. Some light has gone out in her, she's so careful, a nice lady on her best behavior, watch out don't say anything dumb, he's listening. The awkward reserve of a young couple. Each time I feel as though my girlfriends have died and left me still alive.

But not saved once and for all. That would have required looking at every boy with empty eyes, forgetting the warmth and nearness of another's body—thank you, Rémi, for those gifts. Three months after him, already someone else, then the same feeling of dependence. The straight line of liberty is something I admire, without being able to walk it. Years of unbelievable complications and compromises lie ahead of me. There are lots of those girls you see alone for months, they're so serious, almost haughty, and one fine day you catch them off in a dark corner with someone. Loud surprise and disapproval, you never would have thought that of them, and then they're alone again. They must be cracked. And I'm one of them.

I had believed in the *lycée* as a land of liberty, equality, fraternity. Now, here in class, the twenty-six girls in pink smocks seem absolutely foreign to me, more strange than all the boys I've ever met in my small town. Some of my fellow students still seem like children, without any affectations or sense of style, but when they take off their smocks they slip on well-cut jackets of butter-soft suede. Other girls wear makeup and short skirts that are fashionably but discreetly full. There are no bubbleheads or clowns, as there had been back in the convent school. In this senior class, the popular type is the wholesome girl, straightforward, in a navy blue blazer. The twenty-six of them are right out of the *Brigitte* series, from the nicer neighborhoods of Rouen, Bihorel, Mont-Saint-Aignan, but I don't recognize them immediately. I find their casual attitude toward everything chilling; they carp at the teacher and make fun of a scholarship student from the countryside around Dieppe who still uses words in the Norman dialect. They talk seriously about sexuality, about Freud, with no laughter or obscenities; they seem oblivious to boys and any interest in sleeping with them. I feel dirty and cheap next to them. And their self-confidence astonishes me, they never seem to work— just imagine, I got fifteen out of twenty and I didn't even crack a book until ten last night—it's so cool, being brilliant without even trying, I can't get over it, because where I come from, everyone looks down on slackers. And they've all got unheard-of ambitions: psychiatrist, poli sci, *hypokhâgne*. Faced with their self-assertiveness, their confidence, I take my doubts and my habit of working as little as possible for signs of a real inferiority. We're all the same sex in our final year at the *lycée* Jeanne-d'Arc, but not of the same social background. My sisters, those girls? What a strange idea. They're a much greater obstacle to my future than the boys are. Everything my mother ever said to encourage me—you can be whatever you want to be—is collapsing; the young ladies from Bihorel are stifling my ambition. When I go home on Saturday, I seem to notice fewer people in the store; the supermarket is stealing away our customers, so how can I be greedy, when I feel responsible for the canned goods gathering dust on the shelves? Professor, librarian, such a long and difficult path. Schoolteacher, I'd start earning money right away. The girls in my class talk about going to university as though they'd already reserved their places. Not me. *Hypokhâgne*, what is that, exactly? She looks at me pityingly, Annick, well if you don't even know that . . . I can see some girls are more free than others. Not one friend.

I walk along the boulevard de l'Yser to the hostel, 113 francs per month, meals included, three times less than what a suede jacket costs. The *lycée* students' table, the technical college table, hairdressing apprentices' table. Neither contempt nor animosity; absolute indifference. Definitely not all one happy family—different social backgrounds, first of all. In my tiny cell, I can hear the girl on my right gobbling cookies, the one on my left slamming drawers and endlessly whistling "The Bridge on the River Kwai." Often, at night, in the bathroom, I stand up on the toilet to reach the ventilation window: the great rumble of Rouen, the sirens in the harbor, sometimes, and countless lights. The anguish of solitude, the loneliness that will claim me one day. Just across the street, families are at dinner; it's like a series of paintings. A woman flings back her shutters; I can make out green plants, armchairs, feel the warmth. And tonight I'll be reading *The Critique of Pure Reason*. The ten o'clock evening slump. I don't know what it whispers to an eighteen-year-old boy, but to this girl, between paragraphs of Kant, it slips the same old story: why don't I just drop all this studying, take some lousy teacher's job, and then one day I'm bound to wind up with a real family of my own. At moments like that, the categorical imperative, existentialism, and every book Simone de Beauvoir ever wrote mean zip to me. After all, my philosophy teacher is married, so it must have seemed "rational" to her at one time. The next day, I feel guilty. What's the point of soaring in the sublime realm of philosophy, expatiating on the immortality of the soul, only to revel in an ideal straight from *Echo de la mode* and secretly dream of settling down? I'm no better than Brigitte. Out in broad daylight on the boulevard de l'Yser, I consciously reject the fate glimpsed through the bathroom window. I stare and stare at girls barely older than I am trundling baby carriages, and I feel completely repelled by their larval, slimy little darlings. One afternoon in May, my mother and I stroll from stand to stand at a trade fair. She's not buying anything and I'm bored. Neither of us has said a word in ages. What am I doing here in front of these endless dining rooms, bedrooms, vacuum cleaners, electric mixers, while demonstrators are grating carrots in every corner and frying eggs in miraculous pans? None of this has anything to do with me. Suddenly my mother turns to me. Her face powder is flaking off and she's pale with fatigue, but her eyes sparkle. "Don't worry," she smiles at me, "you'll have all this one day!" At first I don't understand. This, the pink bathroom, the television, the mixer. This, which never comes without attachments, necessarily supposes a husband, and children for good measure. So she's thinking about it for me as well, except she has it postponed until after I've settled into a profession. How sad . . . We keep plodding through the dust and the brochures, and I feel as though I were in the backstage labyrinth, cluttered with props, of a play that appalls me even though it isn't scheduled to be put on until much later. So many contradictions.

*T*hose of us at the *lycée* who board in the hostel often gather in groups of three or four in someone's cubicle, eating candy, chatting about teachers, clothes, vacations, dates. Sometimes we'll go crazy, scrambling over the partitions, tussling over a piece of chocolate. Horsing around, for laughs. Viviane and I fall onto her bed; she keeps on laughing, and her eyes almost disappear into her flushed cheeks, so red, too red. The same expression Brigitte used to have in the bathroom, but then it didn't bother me, on the contrary, and I felt like touching, but now I get up again as casually as I can. That's the end of that. No more curiosity about a body like mine. The sanitary napkins in the garbage cans make me feel sick. I don't know when or why I lost interest. Perhaps I was simply afraid of becoming abnormal. Baudelaire's lesbian *femmes damnees*; how frightened I was at fifteen.

So it's still boys. De Beauvoir's *Le Deuxième Sexe* is a real eye-opener. Prompt resolutions: neither marriage, nor even love, with someone who sees me as an object. A brilliant plan, on the way to the *lycée*. But where is he, this brother, as I call him, with whom I'd like to make love without having to go through all that folderol, "You've got great hair, cute tits, just the way I like them," someone with whom I could laugh and share things? No more fear of contempt, of "I took that one around the block," but confidence, equality. A rare bird, surely, out of the ordinary. I hold on, I wait, then the blundering starts all over again that year, and later on—I'll spare you the details, the same old runaround. I'll think I've found him, this brother, for an evening, a week, a month. In reality I'm falling into the most obvious traps. The flattering comparisons: you look a little like Annette Stroyberg, Mylène Demongeot, the list is endless. The first name bit: a face like that, you look like a Monika. The poetry scam: "*Quand le ciel bas et lourd . . .*" Baudelaire, Verlaine, Prévert—how well I know that trio of pimps. And all my efforts to be agreeable, to understand him, share his interests—I really do my best. What I go through to communicate with him, with them: jazz, modern painting, even bird songs with an ornithologist, even the pilgrimage to Chartres, prayers and blistered feet, for an R.C. Just to be nice. After all, what's so terrible about seeing *El Perdido* instead of *L'Année dernière à Marienbad*, he can like Westerns if he wants to, I'll go see the Resnais without him. Because reciprocity, zero. And I change my appearance to suit them, I like you in black, wear your hair up, you'll look good in a purple dress. Docile, dumb, but still inclined to backtalk, aggressive, I want to let them know that they're not fooling me, I'll do what you want, wear my hair up and so on, but it pisses me off and your Westerns eat shit. As far as being a pill goes, you can't do better. Things always turn sour between me and my "brother."

That senior year at the *lycée*, I don't pay much attention to boys; I have more important things to worry about than being sweet and landing a "beau," as the Mont-Saint-Aignan girls in their navy blue blazers put it. My comfy routine at school will soon be over—the class bells, the friendly teachers and the martinets, an institutional setting, but reassuring—and I haven't really decided what I want to do. The other girls aren't worried: I'll see after the *bac*, probably law school 'cause it's all just memorization, propaedeutics, languages—university, in any case. Some girls already know: the ever-popular *hypokhâgne*, that terrifying Greek word for the first-year class preparing to take the entrance exam for the Ecole Normale *Supérieure*. Medicine —well of course, her father's a surgeon. Poli Sci, where does that take you? Everywhere, didn't you know? They couldn't care less about the profession itself, it's the courses that interest them. Me, I run around collecting forms and documents, how to become a professor, teacher, social worker, how many years of study, how many openings will there be. And I could weep with perplexity in front of all those possibilities. Hilda hasn't got a care in the world, sitting on the terrace of the *Café Métropole* late in June. A chubby doll with candid eyes, one of those girls who is always chumming up to others, tagging along when you go to buy a record or a scarf. We've been sort-of friends now for a few weeks. She smiles saucily at everyone, her china blue eyes twinkling; she's excited about her coming vacation on the Côte d'Azur, thrilled at having done well on the *bac*, looking cuter than ever with her waif haircut à la Jean Seberg. "I can't believe how lucky I was," she burbles. "I never thought I'd pass the second part!" She agrees with me, choosing a career is very important, but all the while she's busy craning her neck and thrusting out her bosom, trying to attract attention. It dawns on me that scholarly and professional achievements come second with her, second to the happiness of being Hilda, a spoiled, pert little thing, and that she would gladly give up that success to make a love match, for example. She's thinking of college as a way to gain time. What separates me the most at that moment from Hilda and her joyous indolence: our different mothers, or social backgrounds? Both. My mother, says Hilda, irons like an angel. A homemaker in ecstasy before her daughter, her living doll. A house in the suburbs of Rouen, the easy life. My whirlwind of a mother, her words, you must find something useful to do, and the small business that I grew up with, and money so tight at the end of the month, not to mention my aunties with their verdigrised eyeglasses, one of the discreet charms of working in a vinegar factory. We have nothing in common.

A wretched summer of indecision. Not medicine, that temptation, too long, therefore too expensive, and where would I get the money to set up a practice? Law, where does that get you, and I have no connections. Toward mid-July I get all excited about a career in social work, teaching maladjusted children. It's time I did something for others, individualism is full of shit—I'm carried away by all my reading over the past year. I see myself dashing from hovel to prefab, singing and dancing with a dozen children, "All around the cobbler's bench . . ." In my cubicle at the hostel, surrounded by the slamming of suitcase lids, I soar to heights of self-sacrifice. Then my enthusiasm wanes: I have no vocation. A disconcerting discovery. In Nouvelles Galeries, buying myself a gingham skirt like Brigitte Bardot's, I look at the salesgirls in their pink smocks, carefree, laughing nonchalantly, handing me skirts; they probably never had to choose a future. Like Hilda, but at the bottom of the ladder. If only I had a true vocation, any one at all; I trudge back up rue Jeanne-d'Arc, so tired. I don't realize it, but my fatigue is really depression.

In October, Hilda registers at the Faculty of Arts. So do I. Statistically, a typical female decision, and on top of that, solidly middle-class. There they are again, of course, the well-bred young ladies of Mont-Saint-Aignan, twittering in front of the lecture halls, still sure of themselves, and sure to be shocked by the crude language and behavior of the male students, a vulgarity that is my secret ally against these girls, under the circumstances. But I haven't decided to study literature just for the hell of it, to while away the time with a little culture and not much trouble. For Hilda, it's an obvious choice, in the nature of things, whereas for me it's a calculated risk. Standing in front of the not-yet-opened door of the lecture hall, I casually swing the baggy purse containing my loose-leaf binder, hiding that little proletarian shiver, the fear of having more ambition than brains. Even though, once I get going, I make for the only profession I know by heart, teaching, I still have to make it to the end. Prof, the word that ploofs like a pebble into a puddle, victorious women, queens of the classroom, loved or loathed, never insignificant. I haven't yet wondered which one I'll be like. Sitting on a bench halfway up the banks of seats, I thrill above all to my new life. This adventure, my chance at freedom. Don't blow it.

Finally, they're sitting next to us. The boys, taking notes on the same lecture on Racine's *Phèdre*. Not better than we are, or any smarter. More unruly, some of them, but only before the lecture begins, to cause a stir; they'd never shout to the lecturer's face that he's a piece of shit. Always ready to raise fucking hell—as they put it—in the cafeteria, in the student union, outside the lecture halls, but good little boys once inside, to my astonishment. I've certainly seen champion loudmouths in our café, and I've known meek guys who acted tough riding around on their motor scooters, but I hadn't thought to find them here. Silly me. In a philosophy class, the blond assistant professor looks sternly out at his audience before launching into a lecture on Time and Consciousness; the guys around me sit quietly, pens poised, their concentration so thick you could cut it, not one question. Same silence in history, where not a single male voice, of those shouting in the corridor a moment ago, interrupts the triumphant soliloquy of Professeur Froinu. Evidently, it doesn't bother them any more than it does the girls to be treated as retards by the professor. Unless they're afraid of drawing attention to themselves anytime before the exam. As far as conformity and passivity are concerned, there is perfect equality of the sexes at the university level. But I discover that there are women's studies and men's studies. "Literature, languages, that stuff's for broads." I hear that word for the first time as well. "A man's better off going into the sciences," a girl assures me. I don't see why; still the same stubborn refusal to go along with differences I don't accept. I hear the most amazing things: "Literary creation is like an ejaculation," says the prof in a

course on the poet Charles Péguy. "All critics are impotent"—
this from an assistant in the philosophy department. Writing
reduced a hundred times to the activity of the penis, but I don't
take this seriously, I translate, or rather, it reaches me already in
translation: literary creation is orgastic without any distinction
between male and female, and when I read the poetry of Paul
Eluard, "Myself I go toward life, my appearance is that of man,"
it's myself I think of. That men call us broads or dogs is humiliat-
ing, but then I'm not all that gracious in my vocabulary either: I
often divide boys into morons, show-offs, and pricks, which
I don't realize—along with Hilda—has an obscene meaning. I
have to admit that the prick is the male counterpart of the dog,
a dull sort with no flirting value. Companions in the lecture
halls, pals in the student restaurants, train passengers staring into
space, I'm never dependent on any of them for more than three
weeks. They come and go in the landscape of my boredom.

Four years. The period just before.
Before the supermarket cart, the what'll-we-have-for-dinner-
tonight, the saving up to buy a sofa for ourselves, a hi-fi system,
an apartment. Before the diapers, the little pail and shovel on the
beach, the men I don't see anymore, the consumer magazines so
we don't get swindled, the leg of lamb he loves more than any-

thing else, and the mutual calculation of lost freedoms. A period when we might have a yogurt for dinner, pack in a half hour for an impromptu weekend, talk all night long. Spend Sunday in bed reading. Hang out lazily in a café, watching the other customers, feeling ourselves float among these anonymous lives. Pout shamelessly when depressed. A period when the conversations of settled couples seem rooted in a futile, almost ridiculous universe—we could care less about traffic jams, the holiday death toll on the highways, the weather, and the price of beef. No one's toddling at your heels yet. All girls go through this period, the length and intensity of which may vary, but they're not allowed to remember it with nostalgia. Shame! How dare you look back with longing on these selfish, suspect, childish days, when you weren't responsible for anyone but yourself. No one mourns a young woman's life; no folklore or songs celebrate it. It doesn't exist. A useless time.

For me, four years when I am hungry for everything, for words, books, learning, people. To be a student, even on a scholarship, is a dream of freedom and egoism. A room far from the family, a loose schedule of classes, eating or not eating regularly, tucking your feet under a table in the *restau universitaire* or tucking yourself into bed to read Kafka with a cup of tea. The luxury of patching things up with a mother whose loud, unfeminine ways don't matter to me anymore. A closer look has shown me that the gentle mothers like Hilda's, who cries if you look at her

cross-eyed, are a pain in the neck, because you've got to be careful all the time not to worry or upset them. Mine questions me
eagerly and naïvely about my new life, and conspiratorially slips
me twenty francs, in case you need something, books, going to
cafés . . . No other needs, of course. Buying, owning, not in my
vocabulary at the time. On the rue Bouquet, I look up at the tall
private houses with their old curtains. Order and stability, but to
me it's just a stage setting, doesn't concern me and never will.
I'm off to livelier, bustling places where you can meet people,
classrooms, station cafés, the library, movie theaters, and I return
to the absolute silence of my room. A marvelous alternation. In
the morning, I see women shaking out dustcloths, making endless signals on their windowpanes, dragging in garbage cans.
Their actions don't interest me, they're part of a ritual that has
no place in my life. What do I feel for her, that woman pushing a
stroller whom I pass on my leisurely way to class, laughing and
arguing with my friends? Indifference, pity, as I automatically
step aside to let her go by on the sidewalk. The world they live
in, these women with husbands and kids, is dead to me.
Sometimes at noon I buy a half-liter of milk, two yogurts, and a
baguette at the grocery store behind the train station. I'm timid
and ill at ease; firsthand experience in my mother's store has
taught me that they could very well do without customers like
me, who bring in so little. Clutching my purchases between my
coat and notebook, I quickly get out of the way of the housewives

and mothers with their serious shopping lists, and I breathe the air outside in the street with pleasure. Ready to swear that the most common of feminine fates will never be mine.

Pick and choose as I might among these images of freedom and discovery from that earlier time, they all look like a film shot outdoors, in streets, parks, seascapes—or in bedrooms. No kitchens, no dining rooms. I'm lying on a bed. Book: Virginia Woolf's *The Waves*. Same scene, different book: *Crime and Punishment*. June, finished with exams. I'm walking along the rue Jeanne-d'Arc, breathing in the evocative smell of the cafés in summertime, or talking with Hilda in the little park of square Verdrel, where the desultory cruisers belong to the season and the happiness of knowing classes are over. Or I get off a bus out in a pleasant suburb of Rouen to conduct a survey on housing conditions, knocking on doors answered by women who remove their aprons and usher me into neat living rooms as they shoo away the children. Do you find the number of rooms sufficient? Do you use the loggia? I alertly write down the answers to questions the importance of which has hitherto escaped me, practical, impractical, they hesitate, formulating their replies as they slowly stroke the polished surface of the table. I feel a shiver of desolation—how can they live like this? And then oof, another fifty francs in the bag. No regrets. With the money from your opinion on loggias and kitchen facilities, madame, I travel through Spain with a girlfriend, do Rome on my own. At the

Escorial, German girls kiss the tomb of Don Juan. In a little street nearby, I meet him, he has blue eyes. The next evening in Madrid, in the *buen retiro* at the end of a corridor in a no-stars hotel, I climb up on the toilet, the way I did in the girls' hostel in Rouen. A little square of sky between the black walls of an interior courtyard and the hum of the city, but this noise doesn't distress me anymore, so good-bye Juan, maybe next year at the Escorial. In Rome, each morning I leap the last three steps of the staircase; the concierge is sitting under the arch near the door, enjoying a bit of fresh air with her little girl—*buon giorno*, and I'm off to the Trevi fountain, the piazza Navona. She's from the other side, I'm not sure of what, exactly, condemned to answer *buon giorno* to girls who clatter down stairs and out into the street.

Poetize, poetize, go on and make your idyllic movie about freedoms long gone. It's true that I love this life, that I think of the future without despair. And I'm not bored. I really do make all sorts of disillusioned pronouncements about marriage to my student girlfriends when we talk in my room in the evenings; sheer idiocy, a living death, just look at the mugs on those married couples in the *restau*, they sit facing each other, eating away without a word, mummified. When Hélène (*licence* in philosophy) concludes that it's a necessary evil, after all, in order to have children, I think her ideas and arguments are preposterous. Personally, I cannot imagine motherhood with or without marriage. It also irritates me when almost all of them boast of knowing how to sew properly, iron without making sloppy creases; they're happy to be something more than intellectuals, and since my pleasure at creating a successful chocolate mousse had disappeared at about the same time as Brigitte did, their pride exasperates me no end. Yes, I am living just like a boy my own age, getting by on a state scholarship, some modest parental support, baby-sitting and the odd survey job, a student going to movies, dancing, reading, and studying hard for exams, someone who thinks the idea of marriage is hilarious. Things aren't exactly the same, though. I'm well aware that I was never the kind of strong young woman who deftly makes her own way in life. I was still inept with men. Being pals, clear-eyed, honest friendship, forget it. Sometimes it takes almost nothing (a few chats with a man, a swift glance from across the table in the library) to turn the figure-in-the-land-scape into a marvelous and desirable being. Get it into your head, be pleasant, you're always overdoing it, you have to "lead them on, by the nose," like Hilda, so seductive and never at a loss, but the Machiavellianism demanded is unbelievable. And fearsome perseverance: cultivating the feminine mystique seems to me like an exhausting enterprise that can't leave much time for thinking about other things. I must certainly be too "easy," but then I suddenly turn difficult. Calmly, confidently, Guillaume the med student explains to me, in his room with

Modigliani women plastered all over the walls, that there are two kinds of girls, the relaxed, and the uptight: the former screw, the latter don't. It's entirely within my power to transform myself from uptight to relaxed, to stop being "repressed," we all know virginity is unhealthy, so *come* already, shit! I could care less about whether or not I keep this membrane that prevents me from using Tampax, but that language . . . Word of mouth has it that there's something more reliable than the Japanese calendar: the diaphragm. Fine, but you should hear this law student cackling in the cafeteria, my chick pops in her rubber cap at night and washes it in the fountain the next morning. Sexual freedom: what a thrill. Not much difference between the guys at the traffic circle on their motor scooters and these college students. So you have to change them frequently, regretfully, because it's just not "nice" behavior for a girl, better to find the "right" one, but how, where is he, etc. I can't figure it out, and I'm not the only one. The women's dorms at the *cité universitaire* are worse than the lonely-hearts column in *Nous Deux*. Hélène, so fluent in philosophical jargon, careens from one heartbreak to another. Isabelle, absolutely mad about a guy who never looks at her, she cries in the street and won't even be able to take her exams. All of them entangled in irrational melodramas nourished by the pop songs of Jacques Brel, Ferré, but Aznavour as well, and even Jean-Claude Pascal, since everything's grist for the Romance mill. A complete con, and we're suckers for all of it. He told me I was "the real thing," how nice. And jealous of one another into the bargain, distrustful, we won't invite her, she's too . . . pretty, obviously, what else could it be? The grinds and bookworms, those girls are out, wet blankets; being good company means the same thing in college as elsewhere: being attractive. The ingénue is also still going strong—look at this neat thing I bought to curl my eyelashes—and even the girlish act, chewing gum in class, swinging your purse nonchalantly, teasing the boys, collecting little stuffed animals and Peynet dolls. Studying the causes of the French Revolution, Time and Consciousness, fine, you want to be a teacher, okay, but keep your femininity, so tell me how does my hair look, I'm a fright without hair spray, lend me your long-sleeved blouse for the crêpe party. We have the feeling of slacking off, of playing a role that is intellectually too small for us. It's that or solitude: always the same problem. You don't talk about the crumminess of real life, you keep your female humiliations to yourself, as though you were at fault, deserved them, were responsible for everything, for botched deflowerings, inconclusive lays (you call this screwing?), for their crudeness. At most, shameful, veiled allusions, "If you only knew what he asked me to do . . ." Sometimes we get wind of horror stories: Michelle, the redhead who was always with that guy, killed herself with barbiturates, and Jeannette, a whole pail of blood, she did it with soapy water—

we can't get enough of the whispered details—and it would have been twins. Fate. The man? Free, indifferent, the bastard does as he pleases, we all agree on that.

And at the same time, absurdly, we hope that somewhere there is a man who will not turn out to be the usual disappointment. You walk into the trap with your eyes open, O mad passion, surrealist predestination—I'll bite hook, line and sinker: a man who will even spare me those snares and all that humiliation. Villa Borghese, those jerks gesturing like lunatics at me from behind statues, piazza Venezia, that insulting pickup artist preying on tourists, how come you don't want to, got your period have you, and all those dog-men sniffing at our heels when my girlfriend and I try to enjoy the gardens of the Prado. A man who will protect me from the others, permanently. Time flies, first second third year, soon I'll have my *licence*. Teacher . . . Some of the girls walk openly hand in hand with a boy, vanish from classes, reappear sometimes with the famous dreamy, smug look: they're married. I'm a little less contemptuous. My relatives are asking, has she got a fiancé yet? My parents protest, I have my studies to finish, and once in a while they add that I'm a lot happier as is. But they don't go into details, it's really an excuse to justify my strange behavior. There's always someone to tell me, "After all, you don't want to end up an old maid!" That insidious pressure. I'm not a girl living alone, I'm an unmarried girl whose existence is still unsettled. So, what are you up to, where are you going on your vacation, that's a cute dress—no one knows what to talk about with an unmarried girl. Whereas a husband, children, an apartment, a washing machine—endless topics of conversation. I couldn't care less. Inexplicably, my existence seems to lack weight even to me. The anxiety of ten p.m., the black hole of the parking lot seen from the top floor in the *cité universitaire*. Or at the Métropole, sitting around a table with some seedy companions, prematurely aged at twenty-two by the neon lighting. Loneliness can easily lead to wallowing in misery. White nights and onion soup at dawn on the quays of the Seine, baby-sitting and youth hostels, a life far from the rat race— that's all great fun. But there's also the feeling that this freedom resembles a void. I distribute tracts outside the *restau*, I attend a rally against the *organisation de l'Armée secrète* in Algeria, but it's almost as if I were an extra in a movie. I'm "floating," one of the words we girls use to describe that strange torpor on certain days, the sensation of being insubstantial, unreal. Cars stream down rue Jeanne-d'Arc, I weave my way through the flow of people on the sidewalk, like a bubble of silence untouched by the noise around me. Sometimes I think that with a man at my side, all my actions, no matter how insignificant—winding the alarm clock, fixing breakfast—will become charged with life, take on a weight that would let me stop floating, get a grip on the world.

$\mathcal{I}$'d met him the day before. Some girls—even one of my male friends—would tell me later that I'd made a tactical error, that I should have let him stew a bit. Impossible. Love what passes this way only once: whether this is the sort of idea a woman gets into her head or not, it has been following me ever since adolescence, and since I was leaving the next day for Italy, I didn't have time to fool around. Making love seemed to me to be an absolute requirement for a perfect night with him. For a real relationship. An incestuous brother. Defloration, devirgination—primitive, unacceptable words. Laughter and complicity, speaking freely, finally. The overhead light in that hotel in the Alps burned all night long. In the morning, rain. Weeks of despair among Italian monuments. When the smell of sweat and tobacco vanished from the pullover I wore that night, I wept.

Later, a train stops in Bologna at five in the morning: it's the same poignant dawn I saw at twelve years old. I feel at home in the world. Factories are emerging from the blue darkness; traffic hums. I'm alone, I'm free, I'm going to find him again, I don't see any contradiction anywhere. Still later, we're in a room full of cloudy mirrors near the Stazione Centrale. Hitchhiking on the autostrada.

For a long time, we don't meet twice in the same spot. We pick the restaurants in train stations, the entrance gates to parks. Hotel rooms, twenty francs a night, quite steep. Love on the run, nothing pleases me more, including the melancholy. One more room to be a memory in a future I'm not certain will include him. From one day to the next, I keep telling myself, it could be *ciao* between us; we keep up the appearances of freedom. I'm writing a thesis on Surrealism. Love, freedom. The exhilarating impression that my life is surrealistic. We're finishing up our studies in two cities six hundred kilometers apart. Nothing in his life, or in mine, has changed, aside from these rendezvous that always seem like adventures. My backaches on the Paris-Bordeaux night train in a compartment without *couchettes* are the prelude to happiness. Raw October mornings; the owner of the Café New York sets out his chairs on the terrace. As the aroma of coffee percolates through the air, we finish waking up with large *cafés crèmes*, some bread and butter. Walks. Movies. Bach's *Matthäus-Passion*, both of us on the bed. The same room, now. His, not ours: I go and stay with him there. My visits are vacations for the two of us—no work when we're together, aside from a few required poli sci courses for him. While he's in class I take walks. I don't know anyone. It's my pleasure-city, exclusively, since I take my exams in Rouen. Bordeaux-love, Bordeaux-reward, I change my scenery on rue Fondaudège, rue des Trois Conils; on the train home, I can chart a whole geogra-

phy around his face. Jealousy, spats, the suitcase half packed in a
fury, often, but why spoil a treat that only lasts a few days, and I
want to take away happy memories.

So, then, perfection. The "before" picture is lovely, isn't it,
rather like a with-it ad for liberated women: girls today can't
stand to be tied down, they enjoy life to the fullest, with Coca-
Cola or Whatsis tampons. Not quite. You have to leave room for
weakness and fear.

He's holding my hand in a café near the gare Saint-Jean. "Set
me free," wails Ray Charles. Of course. The only moral rule. I
watch people in the street, the girls going by; we've set no
restrictions on each other, and in that crowd are cunning ones
who will gladly give up their freedom, who will try to catch him.
I hate train stations.

My reflection in the mirror. Satisfactory. But at twenty-two,
behind the real face is already the threat of another: imaginary,
terrible, with crepey skin and sharper features. Old equals plain
equals lonely.

And always those questions, so natural, seemingly so harmless. Are you two still together? Are you planning on getting married? My parents' desolation over this uncertain situation: "We'd
really like to know where all this is going to lead you." Love has
to lead somewhere. And their secret pain. It would be so much
more pleasant, less stressful for them to watch the usual story
unfold, the announcements in the newspaper, the questions

proudly answered, a young man from Bordeaux, she'll be getting her degree soon, the church, city hall, "setting up house," the grandchildren. I'm depriving them of traditional hopes. My mother's panic when she learns. You're sleeping with him? If you go on like that you'll ruin your life! She thinks I'm being had, tons of novels are surfacing here, girls seduced and abandoned, and with a kid. Tiresome battles between the two of us every week. I do not yet know that while they're urging me to give up my freedom, his parents are playing a scenario that is just as traditional, but in reverse: "You've plenty of time before you settle down, don't let her get her hooks into you!" Men's freedom is very well looked after indeed.

The air is mild and faintly blue along the cours Victor-Hugo; October exams are now over, and we are drinking a glass of juice, as usual, at the Montaigne. He looks at the street, the cars, stroking and pulling at his blond beard. Abruptly he says, "It's from Camus: loving someone is agreeing to grow old together. He's right. Wouldn't you say so?" I'm holding my breath. "We should get married. How do you feel about it?" I remember the sudden softness that turns me to jelly in my wicker chair, my unavowable joy masked by, "We'll have to think it over." The future, even old age seem as golden as that day, gleaming with a distant, delicate poetry, the gentle words of Camus. Growing old together: it's as if a blessing has alighted on me out of the blue—and driven every iota of good sense clean out of my head.

Marriage, what does that mean . . . In the evenings, we imagine how it would be. We would get our degrees, I'd find a job in a *lycée*, he'd work in some office, we'd live in a furnished apartment for a while, we'd figure out how to make a bit more money. That's as far as our imaginations take us. It's just another plan, one that wouldn't change our lives, or only very little. We'd each continue to pursue our own interests: music for him, literature for me. The only problem we can see is whether we should be faithful to each other or not, because we've already grappled with that one. And the unpleasant prospect of always and forever seeing the same face looking at you—in short, the usual commonplaces about marriage. And for the finale, another trite idea: we simply have to take the plunge, it's a "necessary adventure," a challenge, even if we don't feel all that up to it.

We both start having doubts, and quickly. Occasionally, we have the fleeting impression that simply talking about marriage is quite enough, an exciting prospect, like hitchhiking to Denmark, but if we never get around to actually doing it, well so what. We want to be doubly sure we are really meant for each other, that there isn't some mistake. At other times we feel our uneasiness comes from uncertainty itself and that we should take our cue from Pascal's wager, spring boldly for marriage, and worry about the rest later. My super cowardice, impossible to admit: in the last circles of love, I want my womb to come into play and decide for me. Making love the way you read the cards: to learn the future.

But the signs of what really lies ahead for me? I miss them all. I take a break from working on my thesis on Surrealism and step outside the library in Rouen, crossing square Verdrel, where the mild weather has brought the swans back to the ornamental pond, and suddenly I realize that I'm living perhaps my last weeks as a single girl, free to go where I like, to skip lunch this noon, to work in my room without being disturbed. I will permanently lose my solitude. How can two people stay out of each other's way in a tiny apartment? And he'll want his meals every day. All sorts of pictures flash through my mind, and they're not a pretty sight. I repress them, ashamed of being a spoiled only child, selfish and uncaring. One day, he's tired and has a lot of work to do; why don't we eat in the room instead of going to the *restau*? Six in the evening on cours Victor-Hugo, women rushing to the Docks supermarket across from the Café Montaigne, taking this and that from the shelves without hesitation, as though their heads were completely programed for that evening's dinner, and tomorrow's as well, perhaps, for four or more people who all like different things. How do they do it? Perhaps it's the crowd, the heat, most of all that automatic pil-

laging of the shelves by these women—I wander from one aisle
to the next at a complete loss. Outside of steaks, eggs, and pack-
ets of soup, I don't know how to make anything quickly. It
would take me hours to fix what he likes tonight: cucumbers,
French fries, a chocolate mousse. I'm surrounded by stuff to
eat, without any idea what to get, and on the verge of tears. I'll
never make it. I don't want any part of this life punctuated by
shopping and cooking. Why didn't he come to the store with
me? Finally I buy quiches lorraines, some cheese, and pears.
He's listening to music. He unpacks everything with childlike
enthusiasm. The pears are soft in the center: "You've been had."
I hate him. I'm not getting married. The next day, we go back to
the *restau universitaire*, and I forget. All my fears, forebodings—
I stifle them. Suppress them. Okay, when we live together, I
won't have as much freedom or spare time because there will be
the shopping to do, the kitchen, housecleaning—some, anyway.
Then why are you shying away, being such a coward, when lots
of girls manage to "adjust," and with a smile, instead of fussing
the way you are? On the contrary, they lead real lives. I persuade
myself that marriage will free me from this useless self going
around in circles over endless questions. That I will achieve
equilibrium. A man: a shoulder to lean on, someone down-to-
earth who banishes tormenting thoughts. Why doesn't she get
married, then, it'll calm her down, even your pimples will go
away, I laugh, of course, but in a vague sort of way, I believe it.

Sometimes I think that he's self-centered and never takes an interest in what I do, never looks at my books, André Breton or Louis Aragon, while I read his sociology texts. Then feminine wisdom comes to my rescue: "All men are self-centered." Moral principles, too: "Accept the other in his otherness." Where there's a will, there's a way.

His misgivings must erupt in his sudden bad moods, his fits of aggression that almost lead us to break up. An hour later, things are patched over. We drink to our reconciliation with a fruit juice at the Montaigne. He smiles at me: "We'll make it, don't worry."

The futile agitation of the last few weeks arrives, leaving no time for any questions. Announcements, rings, doctor's appointment, dress, cookware, coffee grinder. Entertaining, but I won't have time to finish my thesis by the June deadline. Yet this wedding is only a formality, no great expense or festivity, just the parents and the witnesses, because all that complicated rigmarole with a long gown and wedding reception, we both agree, is for fakers who want to show off. We're going to do things more informally, a concession to society and our parents—even the priest is for them, really, "They'd be so hurt," and a contract signed before a notary. But we're not taken in by all this, oh no, and what a good time we're going to have! It's the only way to get through it. Because of this attitude, we have the marvelous impression that we're doing things differently, getting married as a lark. True, it isn't a solemn affair, what with watching all those weddings one after the other one Saturday morning at the town hall—fifteen minutes and next, please—and hearing those words, so worn-out and familiar that they sound like a stage play, will you take this man, and then galloping off to the church where a new wedding traffic jam shunts us off into a chapel (with only ten people, they could even have popped us into the sacristy). The ring he tries to slip onto my finger is too small and stops halfway, interrupting the ceremony. It just won't budge, the priest is growing impatient, too bad, the pinky will do. Things aren't so jolly in the restaurant afterwards; it's hard to feel festive at a banquet when the guests don't know one another. They're so different. My father seems off in his dreamworld as he tucks into his rock lobster, leaving my mother to chat. Across the table it's the reverse: my father-in-law is a senior executive, an imposing, strong personality with natural authority who takes charge of the conversation, but his delightful and bejeweled lady wife is not dreaming, she's listening to her husband and bubbling with laughter at his jokes. You'll see, he'd told me, my mother's charming. I've often heard that said about mothers, but in his case it's an understatement: a woman obviously incapable of annoying anyone, with marvelous tact regarding the right moment to murmur to her husband that perhaps, Robert, you're overdoing it just a bit. Next to her, I feel like some variety of woman with all the rough edges showing—it's almost as though we weren't even of the same sex. This couple makes me feel somewhat nervous, but I never imagine that the picture they make can ever come to reflect us.

The shadows lengthen around the flower beds, along the restaurant terrace; we're on the bank of the Seine, gazing out at the dark forest of Brotonne. I used to come walking here with my mother, at Caudebec. Waiting for the bus in the evening, I'd see the same black forest from the other side of the water, and the landing stages for the ferry. I was a little girl. Well, that's over and done with. Huge joke or not, I'm married. He's sitting next to me, smoking. A bit groggy. Menstruation, making love, that had to come, but getting married? Everything that I've just experienced seems like all those things that are neither deliberately willed nor firmly rejected, and are therefore bathed in a romantic glow. One of those days, I know, that reveal their significance only with time.

We're heading for Bordeaux in a rattletrap of a car. Off on another adventure. Of course, he's the one at the wheel, small detail, you really want to drive, he asks and agrees, as though humoring the silly whim of a stubborn child. I give up so as not to seem like a fool. Marriage doesn't weigh heavily on me, at first. On the contrary. An incredible lightness. Saying "my husband," hearing "my wife," is droll, incongruous, so I avoid the word "husband" and he often says "*mon femme*," and there's something of the brother in that, even better—the pal. My name, the one I learned to write slowly, perhaps the first word my parents required me to spell correctly, the one that meant I was myself wherever I went, that rang out sharply when I was punished, and glittered on the honor roll, on letters from those I loved—this name has melted away. When I hear the other, shorter name with its muted sounds, I hesitate a few seconds before claiming it. For a month I float between two names, but painlessly. Disorienting, that's all.

"Barn or palace / Mansion or shack / Country cottage / With a garden in back," the skip-rope whistles and snags on a heel: palace! Can't afford it. We'll take the shack, the furnished apartment for a modest budget. In the crushing heat of Bordeaux in July, the car clatters over the cobblestones, with all our worldly goods packed into the backseat: blankets, pots and pans, record player, typewriter. We hurtle down dank streets to emerge onto esplanades glaring white with sunshine, a terrible rodeo between light and shadow to find a place to live. The game of marriage is no longer amusing. Frightening rents, squalid premises. The bastards. But we're not much more than twenty, sweaty from our hunt through the streets, feeling triumphant and in league against these maggoty landlords of crummy furnished rooms in big gloomy buildings. The chase ends at a detached house with a garden in a suburb, and a twinge of regret, as I would have preferred the center of town; my former world—university, library, cafés—is suddenly too far away. In its stead, silence, and flowers. And the excitement of moving in: we'll put some hessian cloth over there, the record player here, the first record, exploring the kitchen, seeing if the gas works. A ridiculous house with its mismatched rococo furniture, rubbishy rejects, to be abandoned next year after our final exams. The first months of marriage are like a return to childhood. I mimic the gestures of married women. "Two steaks," I say to the butcher, adding, "nice and tender," because that feels right, I've heard it often enough, and I'm trying to appear confident so no one will know that I don't know anything about cheap cuts of meat. And dinner for two, charming. The tomatoes gleaming in their vinaigrette, the inviting aroma of fried potatoes, us at the little table, loving tenderness, cooking for newlyweds, a Dutch interior of peace and harmony. Our mini-tableware: two plates, silverware for two, a couple of glasses, and a frying pan—less than Snow White had for the Seven Dwarfs, and it'll dry all by itself on the drain board until the next meal. Too bad about the stove top turning brown from all the boiled-over food, and the dust beneath the furniture, the unmade beds. Once in a while we borrow the landlady's vacuum cleaner, and he's the one who runs it, without complaining. We go to the supermarket together, shopping on a tight budget—a leg of lamb, let's splurge—and drawn together by our lack of money, sharing the laughter and sense of risk inspired by our adventure. Where's the slavery I'd read so much about? I have the feeling our life from before is simply going on in closer quarters, that's all. *The Second Sex*? Completely off base!

We've been married for a month, three months now. We're back at the university, and I'm teaching Latin. The days are shorter. We work at home together. How serious and fragile we are, the touching image of a young, modern, intellectual couple. An image that could still move me if I weren't trying to discover how it can gently suck you in, and swallow you whole, while you never lift a finger to save yourself. I'm working on La Bruyère or Verlaine in the same room with him, not two yards away from where he's sitting. The pressure cooker, a wedding present (so useful, you'll see), is hissing merrily on the stove. United, alike. Shrill ringing of the kitchen timer, another present. Here the resemblance ends. One of the two figures gets up, turns off the gas, waits for the whirling top to slow its crazy dance, opens the cooker, strains the soup, and returns to the table piled with books, wondering, now where was I . . . Me. The difference is off and running.

The *restau universitaire* closes for the summer, leaving me on my own to play dolly's tea party with the pots and pans for lunch and dinner. I have no more idea than he has how to prepare a meal, aside from breaded veal cutlets and that chocolate mousse, nothing really convenient. Neither one of us used to help Mama in the kitchen, so why am I the only one who has to muddle through (how long does a chicken take, and do you take the seeds out of summer squash?), who has to pore over a cookbook, scrape the carrots, wash the dishes as a reward for fixing dinner—while he studies his constitutional law? Who gave him the right? "Come on, do you think I'm going to wear an apron?" This cracks him up. "That sort of thing is for your father, not me!" I'm humiliated. My parents, the freaks, a couple of clowns. No, I haven't seen many men peeling potatoes. My father, out in the kitchen, is not the right role model, that's made very clear. His father is beginning to loom on the horizon, the master of the house who lets his wife do all the housework, such a cultivated, eloquent gentleman—and you want him to pick up a broom, that's a good one, are you crazy or what? Period. Just get on with it, old girl. Despair and discouragement in front of the canary yellow cupboard in the apartment. Pasta, eggs, endives, all this stuff waiting to be dealt with, prepared, no more décor-food, the stacks of canned goods from my childhood, the rainbow-colored candy jars, the surprising dishes of the cheap little Chinese restaurants of the good old days. Now it's chore-food.

I don't kick, scream or coldly announce well today's your turn, I've got my La Bruyère to do. Just some pointed allusions, some tart remarks, the foam of a seething resentment that mustn't be brought out into the open. Then, nothing more. I don't want to be a pain in the ass and is it really worth jeopardizing our happy times together by fighting about peeling potatoes? I even begin to wonder what such trifles have to do with the problem of freedom, and worse, I think that I'm perhaps less efficient than other women, and a lazy bitch to boot, hankering after the days when I sat around with my feet up, a useless intellectual who can't even break an egg properly. Time to change. Back at the university in October, I try to find out how the married women manage; some even have children. What discretion, what mystery: "It's not easy." That's all they say, but proudly, as though it were glorious to be overwhelmed with work. The rich, full lives of married women. No more time for questions, for stupid hairsplitting, that's what real life is, a man, and you can't expect him to live on a couple of yogurts and some tea, get with it, girl. So, day after day, from scorched peas to salty quiche, I grimly try to take care of our food, without grumbling. "You know, I really like eating at home instead of at the *restau U*, it's much better!" He is sincere, and thinks he is pleasing me no end. I feel as though I were sinking.

English translation, mashed potatoes, the philosophy of history, quick the supermarket is about to close . . . Studying in stops and starts is diverting, but what you wind up with is a hobby. With much difficulty and no joy, I finish a thesis on Surrealism I had begun the previous year with enthusiasm. Don't have the time to turn in a single paper in the first trimester, I certainly won't be able to get the CAPES, the secondary teachers' training certificate. My former goals are becoming strangely blurred. My determination is flagging. For the first time, the possibility of failure leaves me indifferent. I'm banking on his success, and he is working away harder than ever, intent on getting his licence and passing the poli sci exam in June. He concentrates on his goal, gathering himself for the effort, while I'm growing torpid, spread too thin. Somewhere in the wardrobe lie some short stories; he has read them, not bad, you should keep at it. Of course he encourages me, and hopes that I'll get my teacher's diploma, that I'll "fulfill" myself, like him. When we talk, it's always in the language of equality. When we first met, off in the Alps, we discussed Dostoyevsky and the Algerian Revolution. He's not so naive as to think that washing his socks fills me with happiness; he tells me over and over that he can't stand stay-at-home women. Intellectually, he champions my liberty, he draws up schedules for errands, shopping, vacuuming, so how can I complain? And how can I be angry with him when he puts on his contrite face like a good little boy, finger to his lips, for a laugh, to tell me, "My sweetums, I forgot to dry the dishes . . ." All our disagreements dwindle and become bogged down in the amiableness of the early days of married life, in that baby talk to which we grow so strangely addicted, from "my pet" to "bunnykins," and which lulls us tenderly, innocently.

But it doesn't put me completely to sleep. One day, the scene: I throw it all in his face, higgledy-piggledy, with shouts and tears, that he decides everything and leaves me to do all the work. And suddenly I hear my friend, who only yesterday was talking politics and sociology with me, who took me out sailing, yelling, "I'm sick of this shit, you're not a man, all right? There's a small difference here, and when you can piss in the sink standing up, then we'll see!" He's got to be joking, it's not possible, him saying things like that, but he's not laughing. I walk for hours through the silent streets, past the suburban houses and their flowers. Welcome to the surrealist life. All the immediate paths to freedom seem blocked by mountains. The wife leaving after three months, how disgraceful, it must be her fault, one lets a decent length of time go by, after all. Be patient. Perhaps it was just hot air, something he said off the top of his head. The machine that automatically smoothes everything over has just turned itself on. I go back. I don't pack my suitcase, not even half full.

A few trivial events, markers along the way. One day he brings me *Elle*, or perhaps it's a *Marie-France*. If he bought me this magazine, it's because he sees me differently now, thinks I might be interested in "100 Ideas for Salads" or "Inexpensive Ways to Brighten Up Your Home." Or else I've already changed and he thinks I'll be pleased. I'm not putting him on trial, I'm trying to retrace our steps. The two of us begin to settle into routines that bid fair to turn into ruts, leading from cozy comfort to monotony. The afternoon news at one, the satirical weekly *Le Canard enchaîné* on Wednesdays, a movie Saturday night, a tablecloth on Sunday. Love only at night. On the radio, a voice is singing, "*Z'étaient belles les filles du bord de mer.*"The girls were pretty at the seaside . . . I'm stringing beans; through the kitchen window, I can see houses and gardens, while at that moment, on the beaches of Lacanau or Pyla, girls are sunning themselves, bronzed and free. A tacky billboard for suntan lotion, I know. But I feel that I will never again be a girl at the seaside, that I will slip into another image, the one of the perpetually cleaning and permanently smiling woman in those household product ads. From one image to the other: the story of the apprenticeship that makes me into a new woman.

Quiet entrance of that other family, the model family, the right model this time. They live not far away. Would never impose themselves, well-bred people, short visits, the occasional dinner invitation, a charming couple. The man of the house, as talkative as ever, a constant flow of witty remarks and spoonerisms of all kinds as his indulgent wife looks on, beaming. But watch out, no fool he, behind all the jests there's authority in his voice and eye, in the way he calls for the menu in restaurants, makes pronouncements on the subject of wine or the tactics of bridge. Always perky, his lady wife, never still for a moment, she drags me away, let's leave the men to their talking, we'll go fix the dinner, no no no son, we'll take care of everything, you'd just be in the way! On goes the apron, out comes the chopping board, parsley on the cold sliced meats, a tomato cut in the shape of a rose, tralali, a hard-boiled egg to garnish the salad, tralala. A lively dance accompanied by burbling patter, oh you don't have a Scruffy pot-scrubber they're ever so handy. When she burns herself, she says "Shoot." Sometimes she confides in me—I earned a degree in natural science, I even taught classes for a while and then I met your father-in-law, laughter, and the children came, three, nothing but boys, you can just imagine, more laughter. And that was that. Men, men, she sighs, briskly wiping the sink with a dishrag, they're not always easy to live with, but she smiles complacently as she speaks, as though they were children and should be forgiven their misbehavior, because "You can't change them, you know!" She commiserates maternally with me, makes excuses for me, doesn't all that studying wear you out—it's no wonder you haven't time to clean things properly. I hate that insidious way of minding someone else's business. Her indomitable niceness bothers me, it's like a sticky trap, obliging me to answer the same way, all sweetness and light, puerility and fakery at the same time. How can I dare say anything? So even-tempered and agreeable. Women like her are relaxing, he tells me one day. Attentive to others. As though there were nothing—but nothing—more wonderful in a woman. I had not been familiar with the catalogue of feminine perfections but I begin to become acquainted with the list. "Coffee!" bellows the lord and master. "Coming, coming!" chirps his bustling spouse. Oh, don't pay any attention, pet, it's a game they play: he hollers and she jumps, but they adore each other, believe me, you really shouldn't let it upset you. It's getting late, my father-in-law slips behind the wheel of the D.S., she climbs in with youthful agility and waves good-bye, good-bye, with a gloved hand. Each visit leaves me dazed with melancholy. No one else finds her twittering or her domestic spriteliness ridiculous; everyone—her sons, her other daughters-in-law—admires her for having devoted herself to her children's education and her husband's happiness. It never occurs to anyone that she might have had a different life.

*I*ntentional, unintentional. Our methods of contraception leave room for surprises. Even when it's definite, we can still decide otherwise. The little old lady with the bifocals charges four hundred francs and doesn't look any dirtier than my Aunt Elise, whom she resembles with her black dress and putty-colored complexion. Why choose yes? Among all the possible meanings, I choose this one for the two of us: to ward off a breakup, to transform what was only chance into fate. For him, at the worst, the satisfaction of virility: everyone would see that he had it in him. And at best, curiosity: what's it like to be a father? For me, the desire to know everything, the same haste as before when my heart raced with longing as I thought about relations between a man and a woman. Also, the obscure belief that one must live one's femaleness in its entirety to be "complete' and therefore happy. Perhaps a petty, unavowable form of revenge . . . He listens to Bach, he studies, so do I but less, because cooking and dishwashing eat away at my Bach and my studies, so I'll give him some responsibilities and aggravations—nothing like a kid for that. There is all of this in the "yes." That is how I learn it is possible to want something and its opposite. Just when both sides have been heard, and there's nothing more to add, I start having doubts. I know I'll be stuck for months in a life revolving around baby bottles and diapers, forget the CAPES, no time of my own at all, and as for dreaming, what a laugh. I realize that the little old lady would be the responsible solution as far as both he and I are concerned. I'm ashamed to announce our news to my mother, ashamed of the carelessness she'll see in all this; she'll immediately imagine me drudging and fussing, and be less than thrilled. In fact she reacts to the announcement of a baby on the way almost as though I've disgraced her, and my father is distressed over our wretched luck. Quite a different tune from his parents. I cannot understand my father-in-law's pride in having a third grandchild. I even feel disgusted by my familial womb.

There's the stomach-turning smell of hot milk in the morning, all those foods that taste strange to me. I try to find a fruit or cookie that still has the same flavor as before. Between me and the rest of the world lies a greasy, stagnant pool with a sweetish stench. I feel limp, torn from myself. I read that morning sickness is a bad sign, that deep in my heart I must not want the child. I don't believe this, finding it normal that the body should rebel and lodge a protest against this tenant. During the first months, it seems more like a stomach ulcer than a life in the making. And lo, the child leapt in her womb, the aged Elisabeth in the Bible, millions of grand words, translated into baby talk by the giving-birth-without-pain midwife: the papas-to-be are just ever so happy to feel babykins wiggle in your tummy-wummy at night, you'll see. Me, I'm astonished, feel like laughing at this battered-looking belly, while he seems at a loss, and I can see that it must be frightening for a man. The splendid pregnancy, triumphant fulfillment of body and soul—I don't buy it. Even pregnant dogs snarl for no reason or doze crossly. It isn't parading my huge belly around the streets or the evening kicking sessions that make me feel my true maternity; that sort of pride isn't any more worthwhile than gloating over an erection. There is no shortage of reasons to feel melancholy during those nine months. Africa, where we won't be going now, the way we'd planned. My exam is becoming more and more tentative, and there is a host of worries.

Who will take care of the baby? How much will it cost? Secretly, I'd like to remain pregnant for as long as possible, so I won't have to give birth. I want to hang on to my last months as a woman who is only a woman, not yet a mother, my last days before the six daily breast-feedings, the diapers and the crying. I'm afraid of what will happen after the baby is born; I try not to think about it. My imagination gets no further than the delivery, described in glowing terms by the midwife, a veritable cinch, proof of which is offered by a record on which you can hear a woman in labor breathing rhythmically, every word soft and low, and then suddenly, so touching, the first wail of the newborn, in definite contradiction to the ghastly images from childhood, the blood and forceps, the scenes of agony from *Gone with the Wind*, the ropes, the hot water, the shrieking. To distract me from my worries, there is also the purchase of all the required paraphernalia. Here we are for the first time, the two of us, in one of those stores crammed with enticing displays of tiny, brightly colored clothing, dainty finery, embroidered bibs, rompers, flashy rattles, all sorts of accessories for your living doll. Mickey and Donald everywhere, on porridge bowls, on crib linens. Unreal, this Lilliputian universe. I have the feeling of a terrible regression, for him and myself. Diapers, infants' shirts, toddlers' outfits, baby carriage. High chair next, and the park. You know, says the salesgirl, the first one is expensive, but everything can be used again for the others.

More strongly than on our wedding day—such a carefree day, really—I feel the quiet tug, beneath this colorful layette, of a whole new mechanism coming into gear.

What shall I say about that night? Horror, no—but I leave to others the lyricism, the poetry of torn entrails. I am in pain, damn that midwife, I am a panting, hunched-up animal that prefers darkness to the slightest glimmer of light, since there is no point in seeing the compassion in his eyes: he can't do a thing for me. The same images, over and over, for six hours—an experience of suffering neither rich nor varied. I'm on a raging sea, counting the seconds between waves of pain trying to engulf me and across which I'm supposed to scamper at top speed, puffing away. Two horses keep trying to pull my hips apart. A door that refuses to open. A single clear, fixed idea: queens gave birth in a seated position and they were right—I dream of a big commode, I'm sure it would all be over just like that. It—the pain, naturally; sometime during the middle of the night, the child disappears among the waves. Instead of a big *chaise percée* there are the glaring lights, the hard table, orders given from the other side of my belly. The worst, my public body—that part like a queen's delivery, anyway. The water, the blood, the stools, the cervix dilated in front of everyone. Listen, that's not important at such a time, it's not the same, just an innocent passageway for the child. Even so. He has to see this whole debacle, get a good eyeful of my misery, has to know what it's like, "participate," decked out in a white gown and cap as though he were a doctor. But to be this liquefaction, this thing writhing in front of him—will he ever forget this sight? And what use is he to me in the end? Like the others, he repeats, "Push, breathe, don't lose the stirrups," and he panics when I stop behaving like a stoic *mater dolorosa* and start screaming. "You're spoiling everything, madame!" "Be quiet," he says, "get control of yourself!" So I grit my teeth. Not to please them, just to have done with it. I push as though I were trying to shoot a soccer ball up into the clouds. I'm abruptly emptied out, all pain gone, with the doctor scolding me— you've torn yourself, it's a boy. For an instant, the vision of a skinned rabbit; a cry. Often, afterwards, I watch this film again, trying to make sense of this moment. I was in agony, I was alone, and suddenly—this little rabbit, the cry, so unimaginable one minute before. There's still no meaning, simply that there was-n't anyone, then there was. I find him again a half hour later in my room in the clinic, completely dressed, with a full head of black hair, lying right in the middle of the pillow with the sheet tucked up around his shoulders, looking strangely civilized. I must have imagined they would hand him to me naked save for a diaper, like an infant Jesus.

I proudly make a show of following the instructions of the government's booklet on baby care; the best milk is breast milk, you owe it to your child, but I never get over my apprehension of the second when the gums clamp on to drain me like an insatiable suction cup. But that still isn't how I begin to understand and feel my own maternity, which comes to me at certain silent moments in the clinic. He's reading *The Brothers Karamazov* near the window while I go over some notes, stopping often to bend over the little bed next to mine with a kind of stupefied anguish. I have begun watching his breathing, carrying within myself the possible death of my child. Each morning, I dash half-asleep to the crib. Stories of smothered babies, the covers, the undershirt, fate. Later, I will sit in the movie theater in the evening watching the film through the blurry image of a child screaming with pain in the empty apartment. Pleasure, too: the smooth, warm, pliant skin, the song before words, and all the first times—the toothless grin, the tiny head looking up shakily while he lies flat on his tummy, the hand grasping the sliding bead on the crib rail. Perfect moments. I've known others: certain books, landscapes, the warmth of classrooms filled with my students . . . These moments don't contradict one another.

First childbearing, then child rearing. "Mothering," they say, the landlady and my mother-in-law. That's sweet; mothering, smile for mama, kitchy-coo, nighty-night. Too good to be true. I discover the joys of a day divided up by six diaper changes and six bottles; I try but it isn't enough, my milk dries up in ten days. At five in the morning, I stare fixedly at the bottle heating in the double boiler. Glassy-eyed. That people are leaving for work at the same hour, that the garbagemen are out there tipping the cans into the truck doesn't console me; I feel as if we were in different dimensions. Food and shit, food and shit, relentlessly. Obsessed with germs, and gas. Idealize the humble chore, of course, the choice tasks lovingly carried out, etc., the transfiguration of shit. Perhaps there's poetry in sour dribbles of milk and dirty diapers. On sunny mornings, washing all the little white and blue togs in the bathroom and hanging them on the line, I can see how one might love all that, tell oneself, this is the life . . . Never. If I were to start loving it, I'd be lost.

Fortunately, as a student, he is often there, he can see all the diapers and bottles and hear the wailing at suppertime. Not something he can wriggle out of anymore, no verbal smoke screens, oh leave your dishwashing and come listen to some Bach, no lovely schedules on paper. It couldn't have been more obvious: if I were left to take care of Kiddo on my own, it would mean the end of my studies and the girl he'd married, the one so full of plans. He doesn't want that girl to die. He's not a narrow-minded bully and would never accept my overnight transformation into a baby-buggy-pusher. He needs to believe that I'm as free as he is; he cannot stomach the brutal picture of a dishrag wife. And of course I'd put up a fight. Suddenly abandon my childhood dream of having a profession, the sometimes vague but never quenched hope of "doing something"—I couldn't. A diploma, what a fairy tale, it's laughable, pathetic to cling to the idea of passing a competitive exam, you can be happy without that, fall back on your inner resources, strange that you should have a child and want to run right out to the research library, you have your whole life ahead of you for that, but your child needs you now—arguments and reproaches fall thick and fast. Luckily, on this point I am stone-deaf. What man would have given up classes and notebooks to clean house and take care of a baby? So me neither. And fairy tale or not, the exam is what is going to keep me from being swamped by dirty dishes and diapers, it's the last sign of my independence, my guiding star.

We share the mothering. You take the evening bottle, I'll do the morning one, we'll take turns rinsing out the diapers in the shower, equal priority on attending classes. Not instant nirvana, not oodles of fun lugging Evian bottles or pacing up and down, waiting patiently for the burp, but bearable, sometimes amusing. Never the resentment of being the only one feeding and wiping, and sharing the shit means there's less of it. Sometimes it seems like love. He walks carefully between the desk and the wardrobe, stops in front of the window, retraces his steps. Against his shoulder lies a white package with a wobbly little head at the top. All's right with the world. His hands know how to place Kiddo in the crib as gently as mine; he knows as well as I do how to wipe the milk delicately from the sticky mouth and check the bottle's temperature by shaking a few drops onto his bare forearm. We have no idea how to do anything; we learn together. I have boundless confidence in his care. Nobody could measure up to him, not the landlady playing peekaboo with Kiddo, not all the nursemaids on earth. This sharing seems quite natural to me, no question of thanking him day and night as though it were some heroic feat, a sacrifice he has undertaken to "allow" me to have a profession; after all, I don't demand fulsome praise for the shopping, cooking, and dishwashing that have been permanently assigned to me.

I still have loads of illusions. I never imagine that he will soon find it beneath his dignity to take my place occasionally at the babyfood dish, and that later on, no, he won't be sorry he fed and changed Kiddo, but he'll think of it as a quaint little episode from our relatively unsettled and impoverished student days.

It's true that we haven't taken our proper places in society. My tutoring students in Latin doesn't seem like real work, the cheap food at the *restau universitaire* fills in on days when I fall down on that job, the curtains can stay filthy and the furniture unpolished, since they aren't ours. It's pouring on the cours d'Albret, nothing but furniture in all the store windows as we go from one to another, hand in hand, avoiding the puddles. Looking for an armchair. The material's too bright on that one, and the modern style looks tacky. The first piece of furniture we have shopped for together, the first of our very own. It's fun. The saleslady informs us, in a confidential and respectful tone, that it's mahogany, made in England. She strokes the leather of the seat and armrests. And now a slightly haughtier air: in what style is the rest of your furniture? We hesitate; well, there is none. An English armchair fits in with everything, absolutely everything. I'm wearing an old blue raincoat with a hood, his hair is slicked down by the rain. You can pay on the installment plan, of course. She despises us, a gullible young couple, and she's trying to stick us with her armchair. Enough of this. We exchange looks: we'll think about it, good-bye. Outside, laughing in the rain, quick, Kiddo's home all alone, and then he remembers seeing a rustic armchair for three hundred francs at the Manufrance department store. Tomorrow. Lower-middle-class couple fitting themselves out, following a well-trodden path. It doesn't feel at all like that to me: I still see us as free spirits traveling light, and the armchair, just an extravagance, like a record, only a bit more expensive, not the purchase of a staid couple settling into their niche in society. I feel we're still living an adventure, so I can imagine our future together without wavering. Soon we'll be leaving the furnished rooms in the suburbs of Bordeaux—for what city? He has just finished his exams, and the positions advertised in *Le Monde* have all the charm of a catalogue of vacation spots, at least for the first month. Personnel director in Bourges, community center administrator in Fontenay-aux-Roses, university graduate, Martigues, Versailles, Aix-en-Provence . . . The names fade from the map, along with our hopes; it's not as easy as we'd thought to find a real job. The only thing left is an executive position in a city I envision as completely white, surrounding a slate blue lake set among glittering mountains. The excitement of packing—adieu Bordeaux, vive Annecy. Of course I blow the CAPES, that's no surprise, everyone told me so, insane even to have tried, you asked for it. So what. "He passed, and that's the main thing," and I think so, too. I'm counting on him. I've stopped taking complete charge of myself. I'm convinced, however, that I haven't lost any of my former freedom, aside from some selfish bad habits that probably aren't worth worrying about. We've been living together for a year and a half.

Annecy, lake and mountains, snow and sunshine, swimming, skiing. A tourist paradise. On the last Sunday of October, we don't see any tourists—they're long gone. Nobody in the streets, except for the ones by the cemetery. Our apartment building is not far from the main gate. As I unpack the luggage in F3, our second-floor apartment, I can see cars stopping at the flower shop where hundreds of pots of chrysanthemums are set out. North Africans in balaclavas and shabby jackets pass by as well, carrying bags or hampers of food. On the sidewalk below, across the street from the florist's, there are some benches and a concrete urinal. I go shopping an hour after we arrive because it's the first thing to do, we have to eat. Find a grocery store, a butcher's shop, a bakery. I don't have time to look around at my new neighborhood. My first memory of Annecy is standing on line in the store, did I forget anything, butter, salt, everything seems more expensive than in Bordeaux, and the merchants all look so sullen. I return with my purchases amid a throng of people carrying chrysanthemums. The steaks are tough; he tells me we'll have to find a different butcher. It isn't until the afternoon that we drive out to the lake. There are swans on the shore, as in the postcards, but the mountains look bald without any snow. To the right of a stretch of lawn before the lake sits a big plastery casino, obviously closed. You can take walks here with Kiddo, it must be nice when it's sunny.

I hate Annecy. That's where I get sucked in. Where I live the difference between him and me day after day, floundering in this shrunken woman's world, choking on petty tasks and problems. Awash in loneliness. I become the guardian of the hearth, in charge of supplies and maintenance. What had come before was a picnic. Annecy, the ultimate apprenticeship in the role. Years of just the basics, without any of those comforts that help you bear up: a grandmother to babysit, parents who get you out of the kitchen every once in a while with a little dinner invitation, or enough money to pay for a cleaning lady or a mother's helper. Me, I have nothing beyond the essentials: a husband, a baby, an apartment—enough to discover the difference between the two of us in its pure state. The words "house," "food," "education," "work" no longer have the same meaning for him and for me. I begin to see in these words nothing but burdensome, oppressive things from which I can free myself only a few days, or at most a few weeks, every year. "Want to give your wife two weeks off from kitchen duty? Call the Club!" And freedom, what is that starting to mean? Oh well, sniff the kind souls of this world, you shouldn't get married if you can't take the consequences, men get their wings clipped too, you know, and just look around at those who don't earn more than the guaranteed minimum wage, who weren't lucky enough to get a good education, who make bolts all the livelong day—no, it's too easy to spout all sorts of pitiful tales to keep a woman from speaking up, so I just keep quiet.

That first morning: I'm alone at eight o'clock in F3 with Kiddo crying, the kitchen table littered with breakfast dishes, the bed unmade, the bathroom sink ringed with shaving scum. Papa goes to work, mama does the housework, rocks baby, and prepares a tasty meal. And I'd thought that first-grade refrain would never apply to me. We'd had long periods together during the day until then; he wasn't peeling the potatoes but he was there, and the potato peeling had seemed to go faster. I look at the bowls, the full ashtray, all the morning mess to clean up. How quiet the apartment is when Kiddo stops singing. I see my reflection in the mirror over the dirty bathroom sink. Twenty-five years old. How could I ever have thought to find fulfillment in this?

The bare minimum, and nothing more. I'm not going to let myself be had. Plonk the bowls into the dishpan, wipe off the table, draw up the bedcovers, feed Kiddo, bathe him. No sweeping, absolutely no dusting—the last vestige, perhaps, of my reading of *The Second Sex*, the story of an inept and hopeless battle against dust. Anyway, there's not much furniture yet, beyond what we need for sleeping and sitting down. Grimly, I return to my books, without daring to consider my chances of success, without thinking about the near—so near—future when Kiddo will be crawling all over, getting into everything, sleeping only during his afternoon nap. I plunge into French phonetics, reciting paradigms with the fervor of those who chant novenas in hopes of seeing their desperate dreams come true.

I don't hold out long.

"But nothing's ready! It's twenty past twelve! You have to organize things better than this! You should finish feeding the baby before I get here, I'd like to relax while I'm home for lunch. I'm WORKING, you understand, it's not the same life anymore!" And what about my life? Impossible to take any courses, there's Kiddo, the shopping and cooking, and so on——a run-of-the-mill domestic squabble. Later we eat steak and spaghetti, without a word, while the radio fills in the silence. Voices come and go, playing some kind of stupid word game called Tirelipot. I wash the dishes. He's still sitting at the table. "It's not possible," he says, in a weary, subdued voice. No, not possible to imagine such moments before marriage. I don't excuse him, I don't want to fall into the trap of always understanding, of feeling guilty for not having greeted him with a smile, piping hot dishes on the table, and the annoying baby tucked out of sight. When I start working "outside the home," it would be a fine thing if I even suggested that I was entitled to the same privileges he demands. But he's right, it's not the same life. He's caught up in the system: work from eight to noon, from two to six plus overtime, slaving away to prove he's indispensable, competent, an "executive of real ability." There's no room anymore within that agenda for Kiddo's cereal, still less for cleaning the bathroom sink. A routine in which it is also better to have the table set, the wife smiling in welcome, providing peace and quiet for the man of the house, so that he might depart refreshed at a quarter to two, ready for the fray. I don't know which rubs my nose harder into the difference between us, him or the system.

When he comes home at noon, he finds the table set, Kiddo in bed for sleepy-byes, and the transistor radio next to his plate. The sink cleaned, the ashtrays emptied, the folds of the bedspread nice and straight. The bare minimum is putting on weight. Part of it is to please him, to avoid his reproaches. But that's nothing compared to the idea that begins to seem more and more obvious to me: it's a shame to neglect such a pretty little home.

Society does its work well. Guess what the young couple buys with its first earnings: a Spanish lamp stand of lathe-turned wood, an old mirror, a card table, a secondhand piano, sheer voile curtains. One by one, objects come into our lives, arranging themselves around us. Still hand in hand, here we are again in front of the store windows. Living rooms, bedroom suites, available on the installment plan. We like things that are "gently used," reasonably priced antiques, bargains in the homey and unobtrusive style favored by the magazine *La Maison de Marie-Claire*. Saturday, step by step, hours spent looking, comparing, discussing, not big enough, wrong color, more bronzy, shinier, without the fringe, rather blah, too expensive. Look at that lamp. Did you see the price . . . Next month. Do you think they'll still have it? It would look really nice in the living room, you know. We float home with the lamp. He tries it out right away. An iridescent lamp shade; faint shadows on the ceiling, a circle of light on the mahogany table. He puts a leather-bound book down inside the circle, moves it a touch to one side, replaces it with an ashtray. Perfect. We look at each other, smiling. Of course we know that happiness is not to be confused with the possession of things, we know all about the difference between being and having, and Marcuse, and we're perfectly aware that things are alienating shit. But really, it would be crazy to live in an empty F3, and we don't buy just any old junk, we have taste and we put a lot of thought into our purchases, it's almost an art, so I feel that our esthetic attitude frees us from any taint of consumerism.

And we move on to the stove so spotless you don't dare fry an egg, the gleaming fridge with a floor pedal so you can open the door when your hands are full. To the dump with the gas cooker! I feel disoriented in front of these brand new appliances, but they're fun, too: the window in the oven door, the temperature-control knob, the broiler . . . "Madame, with your Laura (she even has a name, this stove) you will easily be able to prepare all sorts of tempting dishes for your family." Hogwash. Still, I am not displeased to watch the first soufflé of my life rising in the oven, and he is astonished, a real success, bravo. Childish, but harmless, I think. Even a subtle link between us, the soufflé gaily shared, the mirror we just bought, which he hangs carefully on the wall, pass me the picture hook, and the hammer. A charming little nest for the three of us. What a change from the nondescript furnished apartment of the previous year, however did we stand it? Innocent joy. But what's behind all this is that insidious entrapment at the store windows. The imperturbable logic of the system getting its claws into us. Sheer voile curtains, your own furniture that costs you an arm and a leg, for which you go into debt, how can you not "take care" of these things, how could you let them grow ugly and filthy from daily use? Dust sheep gamboling under the bed, the russet tracery of boiled-over milk on the burner, that was then, but this is now: the beauty of our surroundings must be maintained. Harmony must be preserved. Don't I have a fancy new vacuum cleaner with a raft of gadgets to suck up even invisible dirt specks? I'll make an effort—so what if getting the dingus out of the closet and switching around all its silly attachments and stuffing it back where it came from takes three times as long as a brisk pass with a broom. No, I don't enjoy it, galloping furiously from one room to another, from one outlet to another. I feel I have to. Or else we would have to live differently, so differently that I can't imagine it. Annecy is "a position with good prospects for the future."

After lunch, well, *ciao*, see you tonight. Solitude. Not the solitude of eighteen, peering out the window of the bathroom, or that of the hotel room he has just left, in Italy, in Rouen. A solitude of empty rooms with a child who cannot talk yet, my occupation a series of trifling and unrelated chores. I can't get used to it. As though I have been summarily put away on a shelf. He'll have the cold air of the streets, the smells of stores opening for business; he'll arrive at the office and have to buckle down to work, but he'll have the satisfaction of completing a dossier. I'm jealous, yes, why not? That dread of not proving equal to a task, and the pleasure of carrying it out successfully—I love that, too. What challenges and triumphs does this cozy apartment offer me? Keeping a mayonnaise from separating, or turning Kiddo's tears to smiles. I begin to live in another time. No more sweet, mellow hours passed lounging on the terrace of a café, the tranquility of the Montaigne in October. The forgotten hours spent reading a book through to the last chapter, talking with friends. I've lost something I've known since childhood, the rhythm of time devoted fully to a task, followed by moments in which mind and body suddenly open and float free, in repose. He has not lost this rhythm. At noon, in the evening, on weekends, he finds time to unwind, read *Le Monde*, listen to records, balance the checkbook; he even finds time to be bored. Relaxation. My time is now constantly cluttered with a hodgepodge of jobs. Laundry to be sorted, a shirt button to sew back on, an appointment at the pediatrician's, we're out of sugar. The inventory that has never moved or amused anyone. Sisyphus and that rock he rolls endlessly back up the hill—at least it's dramatic, a man on a mountain outlined against the horizon, whereas a woman in her kitchen tossing some butter into a frypan three hundred and sixty-five times a year, that's neither heroic nor absurd, that's just life. You know, your problem is you can't get yourself organized. Organization, the watchword of women everywhere, magazines overflowing with advice, save time, do this, that, and the other, like my mother-in-law (if I were you I'd try it this way, much faster), but it's really a method of sticking yourself with the most work possible in the least amount of time without pain or suffering because that would bother those around you. I fall for it all, too—the memo pads for shopping lists and the reserves stockpiled in the cupboard, the frozen rabbit for unexpected visitors, the bottle of vinaigrette made in advance, the breakfast bowls set out on the table the night before. A system that relentlessly devours the present: you keep moving forward, the way you do in school, but without ever seeing the end of anything. Speed is my motto. Forget the sprightly dance, the loving touch of the dustrag, tomatoes carved into roses; I go full tilt, stampeding through the housework trying to free up an hour in the morning, which often turns out to be a mirage, but most of all I keep my eyes on the great prize of the day, that personal time regained at last but constantly threatened: my son's afternoon nap.

For two years, in the flower of youth, I see all the freedom of my life hang by the thread of a dozing child. First, suspense, waiting for his regular breathing, and silence. Is he asleep, why isn't he sleeping today, how irritating, and finally, he nods off: a fragile respite, poisoned by the fear of a premature awakening because of a car horn, a doorbell, a conversation out on the landing. I'd like to wrap his sleeping world in cotton. Two hours in which to cram for the CAPES. Shouts outside, the squeaking of his teddy bear, the clatter of tumbling building blocks: each time I think, that's it. But isn't he the sweet baby, waking up all happy and full of bounce—I know. And I snap up the blinds, warbling like everyone else, now we've had our sleepy-time, so let's go peepee and we'll take a walk in the park, feed some bread to the swans, and I whip up the old maternal joy with lots of laughs, songs, and tickles for Kiddo. Not for me the unworthy desire to park him in his playpen and go on studying, with Stopples foam plugs jammed into my ears. Above all I must be a real mother, dashing into the bedroom as soon as he wakes up, scrupulously checking his training pants, getting ready for our stroller outing, but not rushing him, suiting my pace to his. Whatever possesses me! Sour-smelling, runny-nosed brats of my childhood, abandoned to the less than watchful eye of a tired neighbor or a dotty grampa—as though I could take you as examples! Your mothers were poor and knew nothing about child care. Whereas I live in a pretty apartment, with an inflatable baby bath, scales, and bum cream, it's not the same, and that psychoanalytical curse—the first three years are the decisive ones—well, I know it by heart. It weighs on me twenty-four hours a day, and on me alone, of course, since I'm in complete charge of the child. And I've read that bible of modern, organized, germ-conscious mothers who keep house while their hubbies are off "at the office," never the factory: *I'm Raising My Child*, I, me, the mother, obviously. More than four hundred pages, over a hundred thousand copies sold, everything you need to know about "the job of being a mama." He gives me this guide as a gift one day after our move to Annecy. The voice of authority—the lady in the book—tells how to take baby's temperature, give a bath, and at the same time someone is murmuring, like a counting rhyme, "Papa, he's the boss, the hero, he's the one who's in charge, that's only natural, he's the biggest, he's the strongest, he's the one who drives the car that goes so fast. Mama, she's the good fairy, the one who comes when baby is hungry and thirsty. She's always there when she's called," page 425. A voice saying terrible things: that no one could ever take care of Kiddo as well as I can, not even his father, who has no paternal instinct, just a paternal "streak." Crushing. And a sneaky way of making you feel afraid, and guilty: "He calls you . . . You pretend not to hear . . . In a few years, you'd give anything in the world to hear him say once again, 'Mama, stay.'"

So every afternoon I take Kiddo out for a walk so that I will be an irreproachable mama. Out for a walk, it's called, out: the same word as before. But there is no more outside for me, just a continuation of the inside, with the same preoccupations, the child, the butter and the box of diapers I must buy on the way home. Neither curiosity nor discovery, nothing but necessity. Where is the color of the sky? The sunlight glinting off the top of the walls? At first, all I know of Annecy is canine territory: the sidewalk. Always nose to the ground, tracking, the height of the curbs, the width of a gap, go/no go, weaving around obstacles, lampposts, trash baskets, people walking blindly into the stroller.

At the park, we women sit quietly on the benches, or dawdle along the paths in the middle of the afternoon. Killing time, waiting for the child to grow up. They ask me how old mine is, compare him with theirs—teeth, walking, messiness. Later on, when Kiddo can toddle around and play with other children, we keep a sharp eye out, ferociously protective behind our bland smiles, in league against the filthy dogs who do their business so close by and the big kids of twelve with their bicycles on the paths, it shouldn't be allowed. Not much more than that to talk about. I remember conversations I had with my girlfriends not even three years earlier, those exciting discussions of romantic matters, so unlike these listless observations about our kids. But is there really so much difference between "I'm going out tonight with Whosis, what dress should I wear?" and "We have to leave now, Papa will be home soon," which I find myself saying along with everyone else? Each of us is isolated by the famous halo of the married woman, so we fall back on chatting about the children, a safe subject, because we don't dare let ourselves go and really talk, as though the shadow of a husband were always between us. The surrounding landscape is superb: the lake, the blue-gray mountains, and in June, when the casino orchestra comes out onto the terrace to play for the tourists, the faint strains of blues and *pasos dobles* reach the sandbox. Life, the beauty of the world. Everything is outside of me. There is nothing more to discover. Home, dinner, dishes, two hours nodding over a book, trying to work, bed, start all over again. Lovemaking, perhaps, but that as well has become a domestic activity, neither an adventure nor something to look forward to. I go home through the downtown area because of the wide sidewalks. Single girls and men go into the cafés, while I enter the only place in the city where I won't be incongruous with a young child, a place for women, from the checkout girls to the customers, with shopping carts so you can push around the baby and the groceries without growing tired. The supermarket, my reward for going out.

Yes, I know, Kiddo laughs to see the swans, crawls on the grass, and then he learns to throw balls, gaze in wonder at the tricycles, sail down the slide with a serious expression. But me . . . Any talk about feeling trapped, stifled, immediately arouses suspicions—another one who thinks only of herself. If you are unmoved by the grandeur of this duty, to witness the awakening of a child (your own son, madame!), to nourish him, protect him, guide his first steps, answer his first questions (the voice should rise higher and higher, then slam down like the blade of a guillotine), then you should never have had a child. The most wonderful job in the world—take it or leave it, but don't go into details.

I never do feel the grandeur. As for the happiness, I don't need *I'm Raising My Child* to tell me when it pops up every now and then, always unexpectedly. One September afternoon, I buy him a red car. I watch him go down the stairs of the Prisunic variety store, step by step, fiercely, greedily clutching this toy to his breast. And that earlier day when he launched himself upright into space for the first time, from the armchair over to me, his little face straining with effort, then breaking into a smile when he succeeded, once, many times. I don't need to remember everything to prove that I was "also" a real mother, as I had been a real woman. Neither do I wish to become involved in that argument of comparisons and contrasts—don't you think that these moments with your child are more enriching than typing or making ball bearings, or even: aren't they worth all the books in the world, it's real life, not make-believe! I was given the business about it being the most marvelous thing in the world, and that's what kept me from going to the old lady with the bifocals. Today I want to write about the life I never expected, the life that was unimaginable to me at eighteen, one spent with baby cereal, vaccinations, plastic pants that need scrubbing, and Delabarre teething syrup. A life completely and absolutely in my care. I have the burden—but not the responsibility! I'm raising Kiddo alone, but under supervision. What did the doctor say, his nails are too long, you should cut them, what's that on his knee, did he fall, where were you? Accounts to render, constantly, but the tone is normal, soft-spoken, not tyrannical. In the evening, when he picks up a beaming Kiddo—washed, fed, and freshly diapered for the night—it's as though I've lived the entire day for these ten minutes: the presentation of the child to the father. He tosses him up in the air, tickles him, covers him with kisses. I look on, laughing, in a sort of cowardly contentment. Hours of paying attention to a child, not myself. As his own mother did with him. What are you complaining about—divorced and unwed mothers have no man to whom they can offer up their sacrifices at the end of the day. But sometimes, in the park, pushing the stroller, I have the strange feeling that I am walking His Child, not mine, that I am an active and obedient cog in an asepticized, harmonious system that revolves around him, the husband and father, and reassures him. Modern woman, in slacks and fur-lined pea jacket, walking in public garden with child. Just for good measure, a few swans on the lake or a flock of pigeons. A pretty picture that would have pleased him, if he'd happened along.

As for him, he has never crossed Annecy with a child in a stroller, shoving everyone—carefully—off the sidewalk while chanting excuse me, excuse me. He has never sat waiting on a bench for the afternoon to go by and the child to grow up.

Annecy is something for him to discover at leisure, after work, with his hands in his pockets and the freedom to explore the whole city. I know only the streets where I take the stroller and do the shopping, going to the butcher's, the dry cleaner's, the pharmacy: useful streets. In the evening, when I leave Kiddo with him and go out alone to a store or to a doctor's or hairdresser's appointment, I barrel along the sidewalk like a demented bluebottle. I have to relearn how a woman walks when she's alone. He must cherish an image of the apartment, our home, as a refuge, not as a place that requires constant tidying and jumps on you as soon as you come through the door, with groceries to put away, the baby's food to prepare, his bath to draw. When you get right down to it, we don't live in the same apartment. He lights a cigarette, glances around the room at the soft glow of the lamp, the gleaming furniture; he goes to piss in a sparkling toilet and washes his hands in a sink cleaned daily to perfection, he returns along the spotless tile floor of the hall to the living room and his newspaper. He can enjoy the coziness of his surroundings, relax, and appreciate the comforts of home. He hasn't washed, scrubbed, or snooped around everywhere like a dungbeetle. Enjoyment, period. Whatever you do, don't leave a dustrag, the Ajax, or a floorcloth lying around, what's that doing there, and he brings me "that," holding it at arm's length, a ridiculous item that clashes unspeakably with the décor. Nothing but neatness and beauty. Two in the afternoon. In the kitchen, all traces of lunch are gone: you can see your reflection in the sink. I've put back on the table the rustic pot ornamented with shepherds piping on a blue background. There's a discreet odor of furniture polish. Kiddo is asleep. Why this tidyness? For whom? Simply so that if anyone were to drop by I wouldn't have to say, like my aunts, please excuse the mess? I've been busy since seven in the morning to reach this void. This must be the time of day when women swallow pills, pour themselves a little glass, or take the train to Marseille. The world at a standstill.

He is hungry. What does it feel like to spread your napkin over your lap and watch the arrival of food you haven't selected, prepared, fussed over, kept an eye on, food that's a pleasant surprise instead of something you've been smelling at every stage in its preparation? I've forgotten. Of course there's also the restaurant, but not often, you have to find a baby-sitter, and it's a big deal, something of an extravagance, I'm-taking-you-out-tonight-my-dear. Not his customary, twice-daily feast, no need to say thank you, oh good you've made celery *rémoulade*, the steak is rare, the sauté potatoes sizzle in their serving dish. By this time I've been breathing them, almost prechewing them, for a good half-hour, constantly tasting, checking the salt, are they done yet, and it's enough to cut your appetite, the real one, that makes your mouth water with desire. But him, at least let him eat, let him repay all my efforts, I'm already adamant on this point, I want that plate cleaned, no leftovers, they're like a waste of my time and energy, and then to have old food sitting around in the fridge, to be retasted, rehashed, reserved—it makes me sick even to think about it. I don't want to lose completely the thrill and joy of eating. Women who nibble, always disparaged as frustrated, infantile sneaks getting their oral satisfactions on the sly—oh what bad manners. Me, I think those tidbits of cheese and chocolate, those tastes of raw cookie dough keep my sense of hunger alive. The munchies, my personal fast food, no plate, no eating utensils, nothing to remind me of the mealtime ritual, my revenge on that eternity of grub to plan, buy, fix: 365 meals multiplied by two, 900 sessions with the frypan, the pots on the stove, thousands of eggs to crack, chops to turn, milk cartons to empty. The natural work of women, all women. Having a profession soon, as he does, won't get me out of the kitchen. What chore does a man have to take on every day—and twice a day—just because he's a man? So far away, the occasional little chocolate mousse of my adolescence, my happy alibi to show I knew how to make something with my own two hands like other girls. Pounds and pounds of food, cooked and eaten right away, sustaining life, but it depends on your point of view, because from mine it seems more like a death march.

I get well into the habit, writing shopping notes down on the memo pad hanging in the kitchen with its cunning red bow, cooking simple dishes during the week and something special on Sundays and for family gatherings. Oh please, do have some

more. My dear girl, it's simply delicious. Let them stuff themselves to the gills and gaze at me with fond delight, she's really
taken to it, hasn't she, who would ever have guessed she would
turn out to be such a good cook, what a wonderful surprise. I
stop comparing things with the way they were before. I pretend
that cooking is nothing, as natural as bathing every day; I try to
take some satisfaction in it, leafing through the recipe book,
which gives the impression of infinite creative possibilities,
never the same dish twice . . . But it gets to me anyway.

Seven in the evening, I open the fridge. Eggs, cream, let-
tuces, everything's lined up on the wire shelves. Absolutely no
desire to fix dinner, and worse, not the slightest idea what to
make. Provider's block. As though I've forgotten everything. A
minute of torpor until the fridge kicks in, a sort of call to order.
Make something, anything, keep going. So I fall back on what I
know by heart, fried eggs and spaghetti.

Worst of all, supermarket schizophrenia, so unpredictable. I
push the cart along the aisles: flour, oil, canned mackerel.
Hesitation. Always a warning sign. Next to me, other women are
gaily pillaging the shelves with expert hands. Others are posted
in front of the canned goods and cookie boxes, reading labels,
studying the ingredients with terrific concentration. I'm sure I
need loads of things for tomorrow, the rest of the week. I no
longer feel like getting anything. I move up and down corridors
of provisions that seem more and more like one big blur. It all

horrifies me, the Muzak, the lighting, the other women's determination. I'm stricken with nurturing amnesia. I feel like bolting
then and there. Making an effort, I blindly toss in cheeses and
some prepackaged cold cuts, waiting calmly in line behind victorious carts overflowing with food and proudly pushed along by
women shoppers. Only outside can I breathe freely. Existential
nausea in front of a fridge or behind a supermarket cart, what a
good joke, he'd like that. Everything about these years of apprenticeship seems shabby to me, insignificant, hard to express,
except in picayune complaints, scattered whines, I'm tired, I've
only got two hands, why don't you do it yourself—this domestic singsong springs spontaneously to my lips, and he listens with
deaf ears, as though such language were nothing out of the ordinary, or simply the recrimination of some underling, grousing
the boss has privately dismissed as negligible and obtuse.

Of course one can keep track all the time: I fix him breakfast, I brush his suit; he should unplug the sink and take out the
garbage. You buy yourself a record, so I get a book. Shit? Fine, I
reply: son of a bitch! It doesn't seem much like a fair exchange of
freedoms here. I keep tabs anyway. Exhausting, this nitpicking
that leads me to spend money on a book or leave the garbage can
full—neither for pleasure nor through real rebellion, but for
revenge. Ever since the beginning of the marriage, I've had the
impression of chasing after an equality that continually eludes
me. I can always make a scene, a real corker, acting out every-

thing, revolt, divorce, forget thoughtful discussion, an hour's dev-
astation, the red sun in my colorless life. Feeling my temperature
rise, trembling with anger, lashing out with the initial challenge
that will shatter all harmony: "I'm sick of being the maid!"
Watching for him to slip on the mask, waiting for the good
replies, the ones that will goad me into recovering a lost language, violence and the desire for something else besides *this*.
Words tumbling out pell-mell with that vulgarity he so detests to
tell him that this life stinks, that I'd rather die than be like his
mother (naturally I attack him through his most sacred cow). The
pleasure of being able to scream myself crazy without him
putting me down with a superior smile, no big words if you
please. But the time will come when I won't allow myself to pitch
a fit, "because of the child," aren't you ashamed, in front of him,
dignity, in other words, submission. A father with a firm hand and
a mother who keeps mum: very good for children's nerves.

A gray Sunday, perhaps. One of
those early afternoons, always so dreary outside the tourist season. I must certainly have fed Kiddo, and we've had our dinner,
too: roast beef, beans, perhaps a custard for dessert. My after-
dinner mint: the dishes. Suddenly, a casual observation. "The latest Bergman is playing at the Ritz." And then, "Would it bother
you if I went to see it this afternoon?" Finally, in the face of my

silence, "What good is it for two of us to stay with the kid?" I
don't cry, I don't shout. A logical conclusion: that's marriage,
choosing between one or the other's depression—both would
be a waste. It's also clear that my place is with my child and his
at the movies, not vice versa. Off he goes. Later on he'll go play
tennis in the summer, go skiing in the winter. I will take care of
Kiddo, take him out for a walk. Oh those lovely Sundays . . . At
three o'clock, up go the blinds in Kiddo's bedroom, the deserted street, the park, the swans. Jealousy, sometimes. Seen from
the window of F3 or from behind the stroller, the world is divided in two: the women he could have, the men I no longer can.
In the evening, wolfing down his supper, he tells me about his
day. Skiing gives you an appetite. "My husband goes hunting
every Sunday." "Mine loves to sail." Fishing, cycling, bridge, the
clarinet, *pétanque*, billiards, they've got lots of hobbies, and the
wives are always understanding, almost proud. "He'd spend
every day at the choral society if he could." And your wife, does
she have any interests? She'd like to take up tennis again, but I
don't know how keen she really is about it. Those interests fade
away all by themselves, one after the other, naturally. Stop bitch-
ing at me, you're perfectly free to go skiing if you want! Yes
indeed, aside from the cooking, the kid, and the housework, I'm
metaphysically free.

As for preventing him from leaving me alone with Kiddo,
making him stay, he has a fine time throwing all my former prin-

ciples in my face: being independent, not clinging to each other
or holding each other back, and so on. Go ahead, call me
Superglue, or something snootier, a praying mantis, a castrating
woman. I tell him thanks, I've read Freud too, but no, I don't
feel like being castrating, what a lousy image. And then, which
is preferable: that solitude, the outings with Kiddo—or the
phony communion of two hearts in front of the TV and dispirit-
ing family jaunts on Sunday to a deer park, a zoo, a scenic
panorama, the fathers carrying their kids on their shoulders
while they eye other men's wives, and vice versa? Pitiful. Nap
time on Sunday is the same as on any other day: I cram for the
competitive exam, still my guiding light.

With two months to go, I opt for the day-care center—and
guilt, of course, handing over the naked little body to the nurse
at the crèche in the morning, and not immediately recognizing
the toddler in the plaid municipal smock at the end of the day.
Hearty congratulations are always offered to the valiant wife of
a man who has managed to pass his exam while holding down a
job, but of course you had a hand in his successes, all that moral
support, and keeping the children quiet, taking care of everything so he could study! A husband, though, would more likely
receive sympathy. What an ordeal it must have been, with that
wife of his. In any case, mine prefers the sympathy. To be con-
gratulated like a humble female, suspected of having helped
me—what a humiliation, a black eye for any self-respecting

executive. Masculine values, the sacred difference between us—I learn a thing or two about them before I'm through.

Checking the list of exam results, feeling washed clean of a year's hard work, wandering through the streets, where the smell of a café-bar would fill me with sudden happiness, amid the throngs of students in June or October, savoring my success all day long . . . That was before. I get my CAPES and I can't feel any joy at all. Too many anxious naps, too many baby clothes to wash, too many pressure cookers to keep an eye on and carrots to peel in the middle of the history of dramatic theory or the modern novel. Another stroke of luck: I feel that the jury has somehow rewarded not my intellectual accomplishments but my merits as a wife and mother.

I am a teacher: the goal of my studies, and then my hope of liberation, of a life beyond going to the park and scrubbing saucepans. I almost arrive late on the first day of school; the mother's-helper has missed her bus. The tumult of the hallways. Then forty faces, thirty-five the next hour, then another twenty-four, and those fidgeting bodies, those eyes, and the voices, stilled for the moment, but ready to bombard me with questions. A far cry from my little apartment, with its kitchen filled with sunshine, a gentle world of dusting and making baby cereal, and the docile tenderness of a child. No matter how I've cursed that cocooned existence and tried to fight back, it has gotten to me after all. I have stage fright something fierce that first morning. Simply talking and being listened to feels strange after the torpid silence of home or Kiddo's twittering. But the pleasure does come; perhaps it's the pleasure of power. I have a hold on the world once more, and even my solitude among those forty students is exhilarating. I am alive again. When classes are over, I am brimming with projects, ideas for trips, the library; away with the bland summaries of the Lagarde and Michard anthologies—I'll find texts they will enjoy. I remember the slight coolness at the end of that warm September day, and the impression that my existence has been thrown wide open by everyone I've met at school; I can see all those different and still nameless faces, some scowling, others looking quite pleased with themselves, and one girl slumping at her desk, lost in a daydream. I'm eager to prepare the next day's classes and to read the notecards the girls have given me with information about their families, their likes and dislikes. At the same time I feel a welcome fatigue and would enjoy listening to a record before tackling my work. Later I might have stretched out, put my feet up. Like him. He's right, you don't feel like doing much else. But whoa, here's the big difference: sitting down, cuddling with Kiddo, reading *Le Monde*—the fantasies of a woman exhilarated by her first day on the job. As soon as I arrive, the mother's-helper leaves. I get to fix Kiddo's dinner, and ours won't appear magically on our plates all by itself. My schoolwork must wait till after Kiddo's bedtime. My husband will watch TV. I'm

not a teacher, I will never be a teacher. I am a wife/mother/
teacher. Nuance. I begin the second cycle of my apprenticeship,
the bitterest years, the most difficult to recall. I had certainly
longed for a profession, the beacon beyond those afternoon naps
and trips to the park. On the one hand, housewives, my special
horror; on the other, single women, with what I suppose must
be empty lives. Obviously, I think I have it better. You stop mea-
suring your life against the one you wanted and start comparing
it to those of other women. Never to men's lives, what a
thought. And yet, our male colleagues can march with stately
tread from the *lycée* to their cars, go hold forth at union meetings, listen to themselves talk and vote on motions regarding
their disastrous working conditions, bickering endlessly about
the limits of their job descriptions: teachers shouldn't have to
supervise the students, or correct detention assignments . . .
They'll split hairs forever to avoid doing one extra lick of work.
Male habits, no doubt. Me, wife and mother, I've got to run. At
noon or five o'clock, they want to discuss things after work, no
time, *ciao* guys, my kid's waiting and I have to stop by the butcher's. I will not be the teacher I had thought to be, efficient, flex-
ible, available; simply functioning at all is hard enough. Classes,
errands, papers to go over, nothing in the fridge. There's been a
mistake: Jack-of-all-trades was a Jill. Do the same work as a
man, but never lose sight of your home: drop it off at the door
when you enter the *lycée*, pick it up again when you leave. In the

evening, pouring the package of spaghetti into the boiling water, with Kiddo wandering around underfoot, I feel as though my life were cluttered right up to the brim, with no room for even the tiniest drop of the unexpected, the slightest curiosity. I don't dare think like this, listen to all of them—teacher, what an unusual job "for a woman," eighteen hours of classes, at home the rest of the week, lots of vacation time to take care of the kids, to dream, the kind of job that's easy on the family, a woman "realizing her potential," bringing home some bacon, still a good wife and mother, too, who could complain? What's more, I fall for that bit about the total woman and take pride in juggling everything, meals, child, three French classes, guardian of the hearth and fountain of wisdom, Supergal, not just an intellectual, in short, I've got it all together. As a last-ditch effort, when all else—and especially serious reflection—has failed, try wishful thinking. If there's a "total man" out there, someone together enough to come home from the office, tie on an apron, and give the kids a bath, then he's keeping pretty quiet about it. Since I am right in the middle of this difference, these are not the kinds of arguments that occur to me. I find it normal that he doesn't do any errands, because men look too silly and out of place behind a shopping cart; it doesn't surprise me when his salary is considered a handsome sum for the two of us while mine is a supplement, a fair amount, but from which numerous deductions must be made, for the mother's helper, taxes on a second income, leaving only a paltry figure when compared with his. So how can I dare say that I'm not working simply for the pleasure of it? I feel guilty leaving him to watch the child on Saturdays when I have meetings at school because it keeps him from his tennis, and I hesitate to ask him to take out the garbage, for what is the point of this drop of water in the sea of house-work? I even try gentle persuasion, oh much more effective with men, dear, and nagging does so get on everyone's nerves. And very important, two voices: one for the students, ener-getic, with an almost masculine authority, like that of those fathers who bellow and box ears at home, an outdoor voice, while the other one is for the apartment and for going out with him, a little bird voice, harmless, intervening modestly, discreet about all its outside life, classes and teaching. The gung-ho, dedicated types—those women are a pain in the ass. Luckily you're not like that, you're more levelheaded, which means that I keep my mouth shut about my job.

Vacation. I take my place among the women sitting on the sand, surrounded by buckets and shovels, while the unmarried girls run off toward the waves, and because the worst consola-tions loose their sting after a while, I tell myself that their turn will come, and they'll be tied down with the kids while their husbands spend the day sailing. I put my faith in family holiday camps, wall-to-wall families, with the two dining halls, the sticky one for the shrieking children, the deadly boring one for the parents, and what are you doing this afternoon, it's nice here, I'm with the visiting nurse service, and you? We breathe the air of Provence one year, of Aquitaine the next; we both sun ourselves, without buckets or shovels, during Kiddo's supervised naps at the children's center, and we dance at night under the pines. Pretending to live the way we used to when we weren't yet bound by salaries, lunch and dinner together, the child. Nothing but pretense. Driving back on the autoroute, nothing to fantasize about, another two weeks that won't leave any cherished memories behind. I remind myself I'll have to buy some laundry detergent for all our dirty clothes, some bread, ham, and milk. Can't you pay attention to your child, keep him busy, he's driving us nuts and I'm trying to drive! I spend weeks in a real family environment. The worst. Gossiping with my sisters-in-law, stringing beans, while the patriarch and his sons are fishing or playing *écarté*. His lady wife proudly calls them to the table: "Everything's ready, men!" Surrounded by this good humor and joyous acceptance of roles, I feel weird, out of step. It's not nice to be so jealous of the men, let them relax, enjoy themselves like kids, you mean you'd rather he were off chasing skirts, vacationing on his own, he must be sick and tired of having a wife and brat on his back.

As for me, more than a month left before school starts again, a precious month to play housewife and doting mother while he toils in the office. I hope you realize how lucky you are to be a teacher. Finally enough time to give all our clothes a good inspection and remove any stains, to take Kiddo to the slide and swans myself, try my hand at peach preserves and avocado and shrimp salad. And to read for pleasure, to write poetry during the peace of naptime. In a nutshell, a modern woman, practical, but not a stay-at-home, creative around the edges—drawing, sofa cushions, crewelwork, crossword puzzles. And where did I read that Virginia Woolf "also" baked pies? Not incompatible, you see. Two and a half hours. Kiddo's asleep. Paper, pen. Anything, diary, poem, novel. Dreading his awakening. But more than that. I cannot manage to believe in the reality of what I'm writing, just a form of relaxation between the avocado-shrimp salad and taking my son to the park. Make-believe creation. Kiddo wakes up. Back to the serious business of dressing and feeding him, then off to the park. Another literature-break tomorrow. What's still best, at naptime, is to leaf through *Le Nouvel Observateur*, work out a game of solitaire, or sun myself on the balcony. Suits my present way of life to a T.

I emerge slowly from the peepee-years. Kiddo goes off to nursery school; diapers and stroller, no more than unpleasant memories. And haven't I waited for this time, my growing freedom, the return of just—or almost—

like before! Made it. A whole slew of things to do on offer: the union, why don't you join the theater club, come to the Freynet lectures on teaching methods, learn how to ski, or play tennis? I no longer even know what I really want to do. I try everything; nothing sticks. Too time-consuming, and I'm always doing things by halves, excusing myself from meetings — Kiddo has the measles—and leaving early to fix dinner. All that stuff is nothing but a break in the family circle, an invitation to domestic neglect. And as for something on the side, a few more conversations might have done it; a colleague, blond, attractive . . . Worst option of all. And wherever would I stash a secret love affair?

The simplest adventure, no-risk, something I can just drift into, is close at hand, and all I have to do is stop taking those twenty-one poisonous pearls in their pill dispenser in the medicine cabinet. How can I have let it come to that? Hardly a twinge of bad conscience before jumping headlong into the only undertaking with universal approval, blessed by society and my in-laws, a job that won't piss anyone off. I trumpet everywhere the noble motive that gets me off the hook: having only one child is so sad, unhealthy, two's perfect, Rémi and Colette, André and Julien, touch mama's tummy, your little sister's in there, what a heartwarming scene. My real motive is that I can no longer think of any way to change my life except by having a baby. I will never sink lower than that.

Eight days, nothing; strange how I don't believe it. The alarm goes off one February morning. Six hours of classes ahead. Incredulous, I discover that nausea has grown in my stomach overnight like a mushroom. Vomit or weep? Now I see what kind of an adventure I've chosen. The romping of those first years, the walks with one hand pushing the carriage, Kiddo holding on to the other. Farewell to teacher-training courses, the union, the snowy slopes that give him a playboy tan all winter long. Endless Sundays with two children to watch instead of one. Bravo, what imagination. He's taken aback by this pregnancy plotted on the sly, doesn't seem to approve at all, as though he thought the initiative ill-advised. Immediately, a prudent distance: "You're the one who'll have to deal with it, chum." No need to say more; I know that in nine months, I'll be the only one fiddling with powdered formula and sterilizing bottles. No more playing around at papa-baba like the first time, ah youth, now the role is sacrosanct, how could he, he works all day, etc. What a silly idea, me whining at him, with that wonderful maternity leave I'll be getting.

My belly starts blowing up again; less of a shock, I'm already used to it. A humid summer in the apartment, the sleek heat of the esplanade by the lake where Kiddo plays with his ball, home through the shady streets; I feel completely sluggish, holding my hand out to keep tourists from bumping into me, weighted down with a heaviness that isolates me from the world and the future. In spite of everything I am in no hurry to go stretch out one night on the torture rack at the Clinique Beaurivage. I want to enjoy as long as possible my last moments with only one child. My whole story as a woman: going down a flight of stairs, and hanging back at each step.

From my bed I can see a blue thread of lake and fat autumn flies bouncing off the windowpane. He's perfect, round, a little glutton. These are golden afternoons; I doze, nodding over my breasts, which blossom regularly and turn lumpy. Curled up in the plush landscape of childbed. Take advantage, old girl, snooze away, let the buzzing ladies of the clinic tend to the huge queen bee, and above all, don't worry about questions that might prevent—it's true—your milk from welling up into the little mouth. Just play with the stretchies and the doll sweaters that are pouring in, and write those triumphant birth announcements: number two is here! And ten times an hour, bend over the cradle to study that tiny new mug and check on his breathing. Really appreciate what you've chosen in the way of adventure. Because it's the last time. I call a truce: I'm not playing anymore. The illusion of a voluntary decision. All I did was produce the ideal family, the one that Brigitte, Hilda, all of them imagined on those days of dreaming of the future: two, that's just right.

Just right—in other words, the threshold of saturation, the impossibility of getting deeper into the shit in the literal and figurative senses of the word. Seen from the *lycée* and my big belly, maternity leave looks like one big vacation. You become less and less picky. Ear-splitting wails at five in the morning, first batch of milk, drop off to sleep, rough awakening at seven, family breakfast, get Kiddo ready for nursery school, second batch, then housework, then cooking—a dizzy pace, not one minute to myself. But how sweet that is of him to do the shopping, "on top of" his job, thanks, thanks. To keep awake until the last bottle I watch television with him. Fatigue. Solitude. But what does it look like from the outside? Oh what a banal image: a young woman waiting at the front door of the nursery school with a cute baby carriage and an adorable child, fast asleep. I don't complain; when my leave is over, things will get worse. I'll go back to my students, who've been temporarily taken over by another teacher, to evenings spent correcting their papers and preparing classwork; a stranger will be taking care of Banky, and I'll have to give her instructions every day. This infancy is the real thing, the one I'd been spared with Kiddo: I am completely on my own, obsessive, finicky, and nothing escapes my eye—ah, this one isn't going to marinate in his own peepee like his brother, during those student years; I'll take him for leisurely walks in the park, I'll be a mama like the one in *I'm Raising My Child*, which has been resurrected for the occasion. I'll have my moment of gratification every week, weighing him on the baby scales. The washing machine is ruminating on its cargo of laundry, the living room smells pleasantly of lemon oil. In the soft

lighting of the apartment in the early evening, I build Lego
houses with Kiddo, and I say, quick, it's time to give your little
brother his bottle, Papa will be home soon. Papa kisses the children, tickles Banky to make him laugh, and settles down with *Le
Monde*. After doing the dishes, I join him in front of the TV. One
big happy family. When the weather is nice, I go placidly off to
the park without running anyone off the sidewalk with my baby
carriage. I sit on a bench, next to the old folks and the women
with young children. I wait until it's time to pick up Kiddo at
nursery school. This must be what life is like. I'm twenty-eight.

You get into a panic, frighten yourself silly; it's astonishing
how much endurance a woman has—they call it heart. I manage to bring up that second child, and teach three French classes and do the shopping and the cooking and replace the broken
zippers and buy the boys' shoes. What's so amazing about that,
since—as he keeps reminding me—I'm one of the privileged
few, with that mother's helper coming in four and a half days a
week. But then, what man doesn't belong to a privileged class,
with his favorite housekeeper constantly on duty? Naturally I'll
have even less time for professional interests and hobby clubs,
things that men and single women can enjoy. Perhaps later. And
why stay in a *lycée*, which eats up my time as a mother with
papers to correct, classes to plan? I, too, will gladly take advantage of that convenient refuge for married women who teach

and want to manage everything: *collège*, grades six through nine, where the work is a lot easier. Even though I like it less. "Pursuing a career," that's another thing best left to men, and my husband is doing quite well for himself, so that's enough. Differences, what differences, I don't notice them anymore. We eat together, sleep in the same bed, read the same newspapers, listen to political speeches with the same skepticism. Our plans are made in common: a new car, a different apartment, or an old house we could fix up, trips to take when the children are older. We even express the same vague desire for a different way of life. Occasionally he remarks with a sigh that marriage is a mutual restriction, and we're content to agree on that.

My years of apprenticeship come to an end without my noticing it. Habit takes over from there. Inside the home, a series of unobtrusive noises—coffee grinder, saucepans—and outside, a teacher, discreet and sensible, an executive's wife who wears Cacharel or Rodier. A frozen woman.

We return home at Kiddo's pace, walking along the wintry streets of Annecy. In the square in front of the railroad station, water no longer splashes down the statue in the center of the fountain. All bundled up, Banky leans out of his stroller, trying to catch the pigeons zigzagging around the basin. I feel as though I no longer have a body, and have been reduced to a gaze directed at the façades of the buildings around the square, the gate of the Ecole Saint-François, the Savoy Cinema where they're playing . . . I can't remember the film.

*J*ust on the verge, just. Soon I'll have one of those lined, pathetic faces that horrify me at the beauty parlor when I see them tilted back over the shampooing sink, eyes closed. In how many years? On the verge of sagging cheeks and wrinkles that can no longer be disguised.

Already me, that face.